Sanctuary
where Heaven touches Earth

A Group Resource for
Those Seeking Simplicity,
Silence, and Nurture

Trisha Watts & Gabrielle Lord

Northstone

Credits:
Cover Design: Chris Hormovas
Artwork & Layout: Rod Heard
Editor: Tom Raimondo

The publisher gratefully acknowledges permission to use the copyright material contained in this book. Every effort has been made to trace owners of copyright. If, inadvertently, copyright has been infringed, pardon is sought and correction will be made in any reprint of the book.

Scripture References:
The New Jerusalem Bible - Henry Westborough, ed., The New Jerusalem Bible. New York; London: Doubleday; Darton, Longman & Todd, 1985. Ps 63:1,3-4; Ps 104:1, 2b-3,4; Acts 2:1-4; Ps 104:10-12; Ecc 3: 1-2,4,8; Ps 119:105,113-114; Ezk 11:19-20a; Lk 18:35-38,40-42; Matt 17:1-2,2-8; Sg 2:10-12; Hos 14:9; Is 44: 3-4; Phil 1:3-4; Gen 1:1,24,25b; Lk 12:32-34; Gen 1:1,20-22; Is 9:1; Ezk 36:25a,26; Gen 28:15; Ezk 11:19-20a.
The Jerusalem Bible - Alexander Jones, ed., The Jerusalem Bible. Garden City, New York; London: Doubleday; Darton, Longman & Todd, 1966. Matt 7:7-9; Hosea 2:16; Ps 51:10-12; Deut 30:19; Ps 139: 13-15; Wis 6:12-14.
The Contemporary English Version - Barclay M. Newman, ed., Holy Bible: The Contemporary English Version. New York: American Bible Society, 1995. Ps 103:3-6; Lk 12:22-26; Jn 12:24-25; Ps 147:1-3,7; Ps 61: 1-4; Matt 8:20; Col 3:16; Ex 3:1-2,4-5; Ps 116:1-2, 5-6; Eph 1:18-19.
New International Version - Edwin H. Palmer et al., The Holy Bible, New International Version: Containing the Old Testament and the New Testament. Grand Rapids: Zondervan, 1978. Revised 1984. Ps 131:1-2; Ps 139:1-3,13-16; Lev 25:2b-4; Matt 11:28; Lk 1:46-49; Mk 1:1-8.
The New Century Psalter - Burton H. Throckmorton Jr. & Arthur G. Clyde eds., The New Century Psalter. Cleveland, The Pilgrim Press, 1999. Ps 62:5-7; Ps 103:1,3-5.

WOOD LAKE BOOKS INC. acknowledges the financial support of the Government of Canada, through the Book Publishing Industry Development Program (BPIDP) for its publishing activities.

At Wood Lake Books, we practice what we publish, being guided by a concern for fairness, justice, and equal opportunity in all of our relationships with employees and customers.

Wood Lake Books is an employee-owned company, committed to caring for the environment and all creation. Wood Lake Books recycles, reuses, and encourages readers to do the same. Resources are printed on recycled paper and more environmentally friendly groundwood papers (newsprint), whenever possible. The trees used are replaced through donations to the Scoutrees For Canada Program. A percentage of all profit is donated to charitable organizations.

National Library of Canada
A catalogue record for this publication is available from the National Library of Canada.
ISBN: 1-55145-515-3

Published by WOOD LAKE BOOKS, INC.
9025 Jim Bailey Road, Kelowna, BC, Canada, V4V 1R2
www.woodlakebooks.com
250.766.2778

Printing 10 9 8 7 6 5 4 3 2 1
Printed in Canada at Houghton Boston, SK

Contents

introduction

Sanctuary grew out of a small group of people who recognized a need within themselves for time out from their busy lives, for prayer, silence, meditation and song.

The ecumenical community of Taize, France provided a model of hospitality and prayer - the foundation from which *Time Out*, a monthly meditation evening grew.

Time Out began in 1992 in an inner city church in Sydney, Australia. It attracts a broad section of the community who share this common vision for simplicity, silence and nurture.

Since its inception, a small group of facilitators has written prayers and songs in response to the needs, desires and aspirations of the community who regularly attended the monthly gatherings.

Over the ten years since *Time Out* began, Trisha and Gabrielle have recorded and collated the prayers, songs and rituals, which have been used in the prayer times. It is their desire to make these original and inspiring materials available to a wider community. *Sanctuary - Where Heaven Touches Earth* is the fruit of their work.

the authors

Trisha Watts and Gabrielle Lord met in rather amusing circumstances on a weekend retreat in the summer of 1995. As the facilitator of this meditative retreat, Trisha intended all activities, including meal times, to be conducted in silence. One evening, however, she was in the meal queue waiting for the roast potatoes while the beautiful strains of Beethoven wafted over the dining hall. Then, out of the blue, a colourful vocal addition to Ode to Joy came from the table across the hall. It was Gabrielle singing along (meditatively, of course) with the string section. Trisha's quiet giggling soon erupted into full bellied laughter at the sheer delight of experiencing Gabrielle's freedom of expression, and a wonderful friendship had begun.

Since that funny encounter, Trisha and Gabrielle have immensely enjoyed collaborating together and sharing each other's love of spirituality, meditation and creative expression. They have gathered regularly with like-hearted people from around Sydney for *Time Out* evenings, spending time simply absorbed in prayer and meditation. This publication originates from those gatherings.

Trisha is a singer, songwriter and teacher who has worked variously as a high school and *InterPlay* teacher, arts director, music publisher and youth minister. She has a passion for spirituality and community a cappella singing, and is presently studying voice movement therapy in the United States. Trisha has had numerous collections of her original music published, including *Prophets of Hope, Take Shelter, Deep Waters* and *Invokation* spanning a career of over 20 years. She travels extensively throughout Australia and the world, offering workshops on a variety of topics and themes relating to music, movement and the creative arts.

Gabrielle is an award-winning crime novelist of international repute. Her gripping novels, *Fortress, Whipping Boy, Salt, Bones, The Sharp End, Feeding the Demons, Baby Did A Bad, Bad Thing* and *Lethal Weapon* have all risen to the best seller lists, receiving accolades from around the world. With a delight for the lighter side of life and its awe-inspiring surprises, Gabrielle keeps her interests simple: "After a misspent youth, I don't have many brain cells left so I enjoy walking, meditation, singing, gardening, chatting with close friends, being with my family and grandkids, feeding my goldfish and keeping up to date with bodywork and enlightened psychotherapy." She is currently working on her 13th novel.

Setting the Space

Creating a space for meditation and prayer requires thoughtful preparation. An uncluttered space with a simple visual focus calms the eyes and mind, like watching a sunset over the sea.

The ideas outlined in Setting the Space are intended to stimulate creative thinking and allow participants to quietly reflect on God in the midst of their daily lives. Feel free to create new and original settings, or to blend our ideas with some of your own. This can be a wonderful way to engage the whole community in preparation for the prayerful meditation.

To heighten the focus of the meditation, invite everyone to sit in either a semi-circle or a circle. This not only maintains their concentration on the focal point, but also encourages reflection, equality and participation.

Music

Singing is an extension of breathing. It is a natural form of expression, used to soothe, connect, enliven and uplift. It is also one of the most powerful ways to pray and meditate, an immediate and resounding way to communicate with God. Prayer can be sung alone or with others, aloud or in silence.

The shorter songs and chants included in this resource are intentionally simple. They are designed to assist prayer and meditation on specific themes. Use them in whatever way suits your needs, adding colour and harmony to every gathering.

Many of the songs may be sung as mantras, the tools of reflection. To sing a mantra is to engage the whole body in reflection, with the mind focused, the heart awake and the body engaged. With this attentiveness, a communion with the Divine is perfectly natural, like allowing yourself to float along with a fresh water stream.

Meditation, Prayer and Silence

More than ever in our busy lives, we need seek out ways to stop, be still and reflect. At many levels of our lives, greed, abuse, violence, pollution, and discontent make us numb to the powers of choice and freedom that we have been given. We need to be reminded to share our resources and gifts. We need to take time to remember that we are valued and loved by our Creator.

Meditation and prayer are the keys to communion with God. When we envelope ourselves in silence, we find a joy that rises from a deep spring. We are safe to feel again. Our hearing and sight returns, and our response-ability re-ignites finding a sense of belonging, and a desire to contribute to our world and the world of others.

The emphasis on the place of silence is a key element to the prayer rituals within this resource. We encourage you not to fill the silence but rather, acknowledge it as the point of truth and a place of entry to deeper communion with God.

Together, let's value our freedom and stay attentive to its Source as we courageously build communities and lives of hope and peace.

Fear not the silence, for we are not alone. Love conquers all fear.

Trisha Watts & Gabrielle Lord

Prayer Invocations for the Land and its First People

Invocation 1

Holy Spirit,
we invoke your blessing on this country and on us.
We acknowledge the indigenous elders of this area,
those who once lived here
and into whose sacred space our forebears came,
changing forever an older way of life.

Bless us and bless their descendants.
Help us to join our hands and hearts together.
Help us to heal one another and the land,
so that our lives may flow with harmony
and our lives with love and deep respect.

Amen.

© Gabrielle Lord 2000

Invocation 2

God of all Creation,
Blessed are you in the sunrise of each day.
Blessed are you in the land and seas.
Blessed are you in the whisper of the wind.
Blessed are you in the insects and animals.
Blessed are you in the first people and their descendants.
Blessed are you who breathes 'yes' to life!

God of all wonder,
Bless this space, the land on which we stand.
Bless this time, eternally now.
Bless those who gather, open to your presence.

Amen.

© Trisha Watts 2004

Invocation 3

Great Spirit,
we remember the land and its first people
with respect and dignity.

May we live in harmony with all those
who share this sacred earth
and be thankful.

Amen.

© Trisha Watts 2004

the seeker

Introduction

The restless search for God can only ever reveal a glimpse of God's full glory. We may witness God's grace in the unparalleled beauty of nature, recognise God's hand in the overflowing joy of a family, or sense God's presence in the deep peace of a sacred place, but we can never understand the true power of God's love. As seekers in this fleeting world, this mystery of God's way always remains far beyond our grasp. However, we should never give up our search, as each new revelation fills us with hope and longing to see God face to face. This prayer time offers us the opportunity to renew our quest for insight into the mystery of God's purpose, and be inspired to observe God's loving touch in the passing of each day.

Resources
• different sized boxes
• lengths of black fabric
• large image of Christ
• medium sized candle
• small candles in candle holders
• bowl of incense

Setting the Space

Arrange the boxes throughout the setting, and drape the lengths of black fabric over them. Place the image of Christ and the medium sized candle on top of the centremost box. Then, position the small candles at the base of the boxes, and light all the candles.

Welcome

When the participants are ready, offer them a warm greeting.
Then, introduce the theme and practise the songs for the prayer time.

Invocation for the Land and its First People

Pause for a moment of silence.

Light the bowl of incense, and place it at the base of the boxes.

Opening Prayer

Leader:

Loving Creator,
who are you?

Who are you who draws me on
towards a mystery I cannot understand?

Who are you?

Are you both the cause of this deep yearning
and its fulfilment?

Who are you?

Are you the voice that gently whispers without words
that everything is safe despite my turmoil?

Who are you?

Who softly sings a song that says
I am perfectly acceptable as I am?

Pause for a moment of quiet reflection.

Song

Gathered as One

> Gathered as one body, we give praise.
> Gathered as one people, we give thanks.
> Gathered together on this holy day,
> joining our hearts, we humbly pray.

© Trisha Watts 2003

Psalm

Psalm 63:1,3-4

> God, you are my God, I pine for you;
> my heart thirsts for you,
> my body longs for you,
> as a land parched, dreary and waterless.
>
> Better your faithful love than life itself;
> my lips will praise you.
> Thus I will bless you all my life,
> in your name lift up my hands.

Trans. The New Jerusalem Bible

Song

Restless Heart

> I offer you my restless heart,
> seeking undivided love.

© Trisha Watts 2002

Reading

Matthew 7:7-9

Ask, and it will be given to you; search, and you will find; knock, and the door will be opened to you. For the one who asks always receives; the one who searches always finds; the one who knocks will always have the door opened.

Trans. The Jerusalem Bible

Silence

Invite the participants to reflect quietly.

Community Prayers

Leader: God of the searching heart, we pray for patience in our struggle to understand your way. Your way is far beyond ours. Let us see your face in the 'everydayness' of our lives.

Hear us, we pray.

Response: Hear our prayer, O God.

Leader: God of the searching heart, we long to experience a sense of peace, fulfillment and belonging. Remind us that these gifts are lovingly given by you. Open our hearts to receive these valued gifts.

Hear us, we pray.

Response.

Invite the participants to offer their own prayers to God, ending each with the above response. Then, conclude the community prayers by saying the following prayer.

Leader: God of the searching heart, all seeking ends in you, no matter what path or vision we follow. You see us all as equals and forever call us to wholeness. Hear our humble prayers this day.

Amen.

Passing On of Peace

Invite the participants to offer one another a sign of peace, such as a hand-shake, hug or greeting.

Closing Prayer

Leader:

Gracious God,

I catch a glimpse of you
when I am talking with my friends
and feel myself to be heard and understood.

I catch a glimpse of you
when eyes and hearts are suddenly soft with tears
because someone said a loving word.

I catch a glimpse of you
in communion around a table
when loving friends meet and talk and eat together.

I catch a glimpse of you
when everything is perfect
for a second in a suffering world.

I get a sense of you
when someone holds me in my anguish.

I get a sense of you
when others help me celebrate my joy
and my cup is overflowing.

I get a sense of you
in deepest stillness
when my lamp burns low in darkness.

Be with me now, this day,
and all days to come.

Amen.

Song

Liberating Grace

1. Let us rise with you in liberating grace,
with lives that know the power of your gaze.

2. Let us rise with you in liberating grace,
with lives that know the freedom in your gaze.

3. Let us rise with you in liberating grace,
with lives that know the healing in your gaze.

© Trisha Watts 1992

fire of the Holy spirit

Introduction

The Holy Spirit is the giver of life. It enlivens and invigorates us, challenges and inspires us, breathing the breath of creativity and joy into our lives. When we are blessed with the Holy Spirit, we experience the same power that transformed the apostles during Pentecost, an extraordinary fire from within that spurs us to new and greater heights in serving God and others. This fire awakens the countless gifts that have been given to us, helping us to become people fully alive. This prayer time offers us the opportunity to realise the immeasurable potential that our gifts hold, and pray that we may use them in the same way the apostles did, to change ourselves and our world for the better.

Resources

- fire-pot
- length of orange fabric
- red candles

Setting the Space

Use the length of orange fabric to construct a circle, and place the fire-pot in its centre. Position some red candles around the perimeter of the circle and light them. Then, when instructed, light a small fire in the fire-pot.

fire of the Holy spirit

Welcome

When the participants are ready, offer them a warm greeting. Then, introduce the theme and practise the songs for the prayer time.

Invocation for the Land and its First People

Pause for a moment of silence.

Song

Holy Fire

> Holy Fire Spirit,
> create in us this day
> a spark in which to kindle
> love and play.
>
> © Trisha Watts 2002

Opening Prayer

> *Leader:*
>
> Fire of Heaven,
> it is your love that unites us
> and has gathered us here together.
> Open our eyes to the gifts
> you have embodied in us,
> so that we may express them, and in so doing,
> express the truest part of ourselves,
> thereby releasing our greatest joy.
>
> Amen.

Psalm

Psalm 104:1,2b-3,4

Bless Yahweh, my God,
how great you are!
You stretch out the heavens like a tent,
build your palace on the waters above,
appointing the winds your messengers,
flames of fire your servants.

Trans. The New Jerusalem Bible

Reading

Acts 2:1-4

When Pentecost day came around, they had all met together,
when suddenly there came from heaven a sound as of a violent
wind which filled the entire house in which they were sitting;
and there appeared to them tongues as of fire; these separated
and came to rest on the head of each of them. They were all
filled with the Holy Spirit and began to speak different lan-
guages as the Spirit gave them power to express themselves.

Trans. The New Jerusalem Bible

Light the fire in the fire-pot.

Silence

Invite the participants to reflect quietly.

fire of the Holy spirit

Reflection

Hildegard of Bingen (1098-1179)

Holy Spirit,
giving life to all life,
moving all creatures,
root of all things,
washing them clean,
wiping out their mistakes,
healing their wounds,
you are our true life,
luminous, wonderful,
awakening the heart
from its ancient sleep.

Ref. Stephen Mitchell, The Enlightened Heart. (USA: Harper Perennial, 1993), 42.

Song

The Wind Blows

The wind blows where it wills;
you know not where it's coming from or where it's going to.
The wind blows where it wills;
you know not where it's coming from or where it's going to.

So too are those, those who are born of the Spirit.
So too are those, those who are born of the Spirit.

© Trisha Watts 1995

Silence

Invite the participants to reflect quietly.

Community Prayers

Leader: Holy Spirit, we take time to pause and remember the needs of our community and our world.

We remember those who long for healing in body, mind and soul.

Be their hope, we pray.

Response: Come, O Breath of Life.

Leader: We remember infants in children's hospitals, teenagers in youth hostels and the aged in nursing homes.
Be their friends, we pray.

Response.

Leader: We remember our parents, teachers and leaders.
May your inspiring, stirring presence help them to make life–giving choices for those in their care.

Be their guide, we pray.

Response.

Invite the participants to offer their own prayers to God, concluding each with the above response. Then, conclude the community prayers by saying the following prayer.

Leader: Loving God, we thank you for the gift of your Spirit, as companion, inspirer, healer, comforter and guide. We gather all these prayers in the joy of the Spirit's presence amongst us.

Amen.

Song

Give Us Courage

1. Holy Spirit, teach us to forgive.
   Holy Spirit, free us now to live.

Chorus:
Give us courage to face each day.
Give us wisdom in all we do and say.
Holy Spirit, teach us to forgive.

2. Holy Spirit, we turn our eyes to you.
   Holy Spirit, your flame of love renews!

Chorus.

© Trisha Watts & Monica O'Brien 2001

Closing Prayer

All:

Beautiful Spirit,
you call to us with a soft and gentle voice.
Sometimes we don't hear you.

Awaken our ears,
our eyes, our hearts
to your fiery knowledge.
Make us part of the circuitry
that brings fire from heaven.
Make us aware of your continuous presence,
even in our darkest night.

Stay with us forever.

Amen.

wilderness

Introduction

In the wilderness, far from the city's occasional bleakness, we can experience the true freedom of God's love. Here, in a paradise of life and beauty, every creature, every plant, every mountain, every valley sings out with one voice, urging us to let our hearts soar. Every creation of God beckons us to breathe deeply and liberate ourselves from our rigid daily schedules, the ill-fitting templates which leave so many things of real value unattended and forgotten. This prayer time offers us the opportunity to rediscover the freedom God has given us, rising to the challenge of nature with an inexhaustible enthusiasm and playfulness.

Setting the Space

This liturgy suits an outdoor bushland setting.

Lay the length of coloured fabric in the centre of the space. Place the bowls of foliage, feathers and seeds on the fabric and scatter the tea lights throughout the setting. It may be necessary to use candle holders to protect the tea lights from wind. Position the cushions, chairs and blankets in a circle around the length of fabric. Light the tea lights.

Resources

- length of coloured fabric
- large wooden bowl containing foliage such as leaves, flowers and twigs
- bowl of feathers
- bowl of native plant seeds
- several tea lights
- candle holders
- cushions, blankets and fold-up chairs
- drums or other percussion instruments

wilderness

Welcome

When the participants are ready, offer them a warm greeting. Then, introduce the theme and practise the songs for the prayer time.

Invocation for the Land and its First People

Lift up the bowls of feathers and seeds.

Pause for a moment of silence.

Opening Prayer

> ### Leader:
>
> Wild,
> unnameable,
> untameable Spirit,
> your passionate presence
> inspires and delights us.
>
> With your raging rapids,
> towering mountains
> and belching fires,
> you call to our wild first nature.
>
> Come, liberate us
> from our self-imposed limitations,
> so that we may be open
> to explore, recognise
> and connect with your freedom.
>
> Amen.

Song

Rest and Wait

Rest and wait in the wilderness.
Listen and see with your heart.

© Trisha Watts 1993

Silence

Invite the participants to reflect quietly.

Guided Meditation

Leader (slowly and reflectively):

Breathe in the environment around you.

With your eyes open or closed,
ground yourself on this earth.

Feel the wind,
the light,
and the warmth/coolness on your skin.

Smell the air and listen to the bush.

Open yourself to this space,
aware of the outer and inner wilderness.

Pause for a moment of silence.

Canticle for the Wilderness

Divide the participants into two groups, A and B. Ask each group to say alternate lines of the canticle, before joining together for the final line.

A. Praise be to God for the wilderness.

B. Praise be to God for the abundance of the earth.

A. Praise be to God for its many creatures: lichens, mosses, ants and bees.

B. Praise be to God for canyons, gorges, cliffs and rivers.

A. Praise be to God for the scent of flowers and the colours of birds.

B. Praise be to God for changing light and dancing shadows.

A. Praise be to God for the distant skies and the wild winds.

All: Praise be to God for our place in all creation.

Courtesy of the Chester Street Arts Workshop, Epping, Sydney.

Psalm

Psalm 104:10-12

In the ravines you opened up springs,
running down between the mountains,
supplying water for all the wild beasts;
the wild asses quench their thirst,
on their banks the birds of the air make their nests,
they sing among the leaves.

Trans. The New Jerusalem Bible

Reading

Hosea 2:16

I am going to lure her
and lead her out into the wilderness
and speak to her heart.

Trans. The Jerusalem Bible

Silence

Invite the participants to reflect quietly.

Community Prayers

Leader: Creator God, you made the creatures of the wilderness: mammals and birds, flying and creeping insects, worms and arthropods.

For this, we give thanks.

Response: Giver of Life, Alleluia!

Leader: Creator God, you give us the resources which sustain life: food to eat, water to drink and air to breathe.

For this, we give thanks.

Response.

Leader: Creator God, you provide a feast of wild delights, a banquet with enough for all. Your providence is generous and abundant.

For this, we give thanks.

Response.

Leader: Creator God, your rivers once flowed unpolluted, fresh with streams full of fish. You have made us stewards of your creation. Help us to restore our waterways.

For this, we seek foresight.

Response: Giver of Life, hear us.

Leader: Creator God, the breathtaking beauty of the rugged wilderness reminds us of the mystery of your presence and the interconnectedness of all of life. May we be advocates for the protection and conservation of wildlife in its many forms.

For this, we seek vision.

Response.

Leader: Creator God, the earth sustains a multitude of living things which are meant to be shared and cared for equally. There are enough resources to feed the hungry and nourish the poor. Stir us to a radical hospitality.

For this, we seek generosity.
Response.

Invite the participants to offer their own prayers to God. Then, conclude the community prayers by saying the following prayer.

Leader: Creator God, we offer to you the prayers and concerns of our hearts. We know that you hear us and are with us.

Amen.

Pass the bowl of seeds around the circle, and invite the participants to each take a seed to plant as a symbol of stewardship.

Song

Like a Tree

Like a tree that stands by the stream,
send deep your roots to the water.
Be not afraid of the weather that comes.
You will bear fruit if you trust in my love.

© Trisha Watts 1993

Invite the participants to stand together.

The Wilderness Creed

All:

I believe in the wilderness.
I believe in the interdependence of all living things.
I believe in the grandeur of the great and tiny,
in the scorched and fresh earth.
I believe in the space that allows our hearts to soar,
the room to move and breathe.

I believe that the wilderness reminds us to live in freedom,
revealing the mysteries of death and rebirth.
I believe that the wilderness is a great sanctuary
of playfulness, creativity and celebration.
I believe that the wilderness surprises us
when we have reached the end of our possibilities.

I believe in the power of the wilderness
to transform itself after destruction,
providing us with an example of renewal and hope.

Courtesy of the Chester Street Arts Workshop, Epping, Sydney.

Pass the bowl of feathers around the circle and invite the participants to each take one as a symbol of freedom. Then, encourage them to link hands and join in the singing of the following song. They may wish to use drums or other percussion instruments to accompany the song.

Song

Wild Spirit

> Speak to my heart, wild Spirit.
> Speak to my heart, wild Spirit.
>
> © Trisha Watts 2003

Closing Prayer

> *Leader:*
>
> Go out in confidence,
> delighting in the sun on your shoulders,
> feeling the wind in your hair,
> touching the earth beneath your feet,
> knowing that our generous, abundant God
> walks with you always.
>
> Amen.

holy paradox

Introduction

The mystery of God's way is the only truly unfathomable mystery in this world. Humankind may soar to immense heights in science and philosophy, discover the patterns and progress of life, and understand the intimate workings of the universe, but the breadth of God's love will always remain inconceivable. This is the Holy Paradox: the mystery of God's great plan for us, something that we can never control or fully understand. This prayer time offers us the opportunity to give thanks for the mysteries that have been revealed to us and those that remain beyond our comprehension, and place our faith in God to guide us along the sacred path.

> **Resources**
>
> - string
> - three tall stands
> - two lengths of black fabric
> - two lengths of white fabric
> - large candle
> - small box
> - tea lights
> - cross
> - symbols which indicate opposites (see the 'Litany of Polarities' below)

Setting the Space

Fix the string like a clothes line between two stands, and hang on it one length each of black and white fabric. Cover the remaining stand with the second length of white fabric, and place it in front of the hanging black fabric. Then, place the large candle on top of the stand. Cover the small box with the second length of black fabric, and place it in front of the hanging white fabric. Then, position some tea lights on top of the small box and around its base, and light them. Finally, lean the cross against the tall stand and the symbols representing opposites against the small box.

holy paradox

Welcome

When the participants are ready, offer them a warm greeting.
Then, introduce the theme and practise the songs for the prayer time.

Invocation for the Land and its First People

Pause for a moment of silence.

Opening Prayer

> ### Leader:
>
> Holy Spirit,
> teach us, gathered here,
> how to learn your truths;
> that yes and no exist
> side by side
> in this world,
> in us,
> and in life and death.
>
> Amen.

Song

Praying as One

> 1. Gathered as one,
>   unfold in us your mysteries.
>   Gathered as one,
>   enfold us in your grace.
>
> 2. Praying as one,
>   you call us to our fullness.
>   Praying as one,
>   you heal and make us whole.

© Trisha Watts 2003

Litany of Polarities

Leader: Blessed be God for alpha and omega, moon and sun, yin and yang, male and female.

Response: Blessed be God.

Leader: For black and white, land and sea, high and low, loud and soft.

Response.

Leader: For young and old, large and small, cats and dogs.
Response.

Leader: For sweet and sour, hot and cold, left and right.
Response.

Leader: For summer and winter, light and dark, hello and goodbye, separation and union.

Response.

Leader: For north and south, day and night, in and out.

Response.

Leader: For wet and dry, opening and closing, yes and no.

Response.

Leader: For contraction and expansion, strength and weakness, poverty and plenty.

Response.

Leader: For earth and sky, laughter and tears, consciousness and unconsciousness.

Response.
Leader: Loving God, for all these polarities, we give you thanks.

All: Amen.

Reading

Ecclesiastes: 3:1-2,4,8

There is a season for everything, a time for every occupation under heaven:

A time for giving birth,
a time for dying;
a time for planting,
a time for uprooting what has been planted.

A time for tears,
a time for laughter;
a time for mourning,
a time for dancing.

A time for loving,
a time for hating;
a time for war,
a time for peace.

Trans. The New Jerusalem Bible

Song

Yielding

Unfolding love,
open and free,
lavishly given,
yielding mystery.

© Trisha Watts 1995

Silence

Invite the participants to reflect quietly.

Reflections

Albert Einstein

The most beautiful experience we can have is the mysterious.

www.quotationspage.com/quote/1388. Accessed Dec 20, 2004.

Sue Richter

Opposites are not fixed.
They break down and collapse into each other,
revealing a central paradox that one is dependent on the other
for its meaning.

Whiteblack:red. Art Exhibition, 24 Hour Art, Northern Territory Centre for Contemporary Art.

Silence

Invite the participants to reflect quietly.

Community Prayers

Leader: Enfolding God, we pause to remember our world. We pray for those whose eyes are tired and have seen too much of the world's pain. May they find images of beauty and hope.

Response: Grant this, O God.

Leader: We pray for those whose ears hear only what they want to hear. May they learn to listen to the truth of others' stories.
Response.

Leader: We pray for those whose mouths cannot tell their stories of trauma and violence. May they be encouraged to speak in safe environments.

Response.

Leader: We pray for those whose hands have caused destruction. May healing turn them towards service and rebuilding.
Response.

Leader: We pray for those whose feet have crushed the backs of others. May they find pleasure in walking towards peace and reconciliation.

Response.

Leader: We pray for those whose hearts have closed down, unable to receive or give love. May they open themselves to your unconditional love.

Response.

Invite the participants to pray in a similar manner to the above.
Then, gather the prayers of all present by saying the following prayer.

Leader: Enfolding God, we offer to you all the prayers and concerns of our hearts, knowing that you lovingly hear us.

Amen.

Song

A Time for Every Season

Chorus:

There is a time for ev'ry season under heaven.
There is a time for ev'ry season under heaven.

1. A time for birthing, a time for dying;
   A time for uprooting, a time to plant;
   A time for killing, a time for healing;
   A time for ev'rything.

Chorus.

2. A time for weeping, a time for laughing;
   A time for mourning, a time to dance;
   A time for searching, a time for losing;
   A time for ev'rything.

Chorus.

3. A time for tearing, a time for mending;
   A time for silence, a time to speak;
   A time for loving, a time for hating;
   A time for ev'rything.

Chorus.

© Trisha Watts 2002

Closing Prayer

Leader:

Holy Paradox,
you are the bridge
which helps us to cross
unfathomable voids,
translating the incomprehensible
through the key of your love.

Teach us to love and honour
every aspect of our lives,
growing in wisdom and understanding
until we reach this world's last great paradox;
death and new life in a world without end.

Amen.

the undivided heart

Introduction

Our hearts are often divided between the choice of right or wrong. We are offered the choice to enter into God's saving love, and yet our bitterness and anger hold us back. Our hurt and suffering cloud our vision, spoiling the promise of a reconciled future with the scars of the past. In these times, we need to model our hearts on the undivided heart of God. When we are torn between the desire to forgive and the selfish refusal to forget, we need to choose reconciliation, new life and new love. This prayer time offers us the opportunity to release our hold on resentment, so that we may forgive ourselves and others of any wrongs and confidently step forward in our lives.

Resources

- several long lengths of red, crimson and pink fabric

- twenty tea lights and tea light holders

- four medium-sized candles

- large candle

- one stone for each participant

Setting the Space

Twist and overlap the lengths of fabric into the shape of a heart, and position it in the centre of the space. Then, place the tea lights in their holders and arrange them on the folds of the fabric, with the large candle in the centre of the heart. Position the four medium-sized candles around the large candle, and place a pile of stones at the base of the heart. Ensure that there is one stone for each participant. Finally, light the tea lights and the four surrounding candles.

the undivided heart

Welcome

When the participants are ready, offer them a warm greeting.
Then, introduce the theme and practise the songs for the prayer time.

Invocation for the Land and its First People.

Pause for a moment of silence.

Song

Rest and Wait

Rest and wait in the wilderness.
Listen and see with your heart.

© Trisha Watts 1995

Opening Prayer

Leader:

Holy Spirit,
in this space,
we enter your undivided heart.

To you,
each of us brings our divided self,
our lack of love,
our harsh judgements of self and others,
our hatreds
and our pitilessness.

You know that we are sometimes vengeful in our minds,
split from our own hearts.
Sometimes we don't want to forgive.

Sometimes we want to maintain our resentments,
to hold on to our anger.

Yet you never judge us harshly,
holding us in your love
until we are ready to release our burdens.

In this sacred space,
we sense your welcoming love
and your open arms enfolding us.
We bless you, Comforter,
for your eternal patience.

Deep within this precious moment,
may we feel our own divided hearts mend,
embracing ourselves,
all people,
all situations,
and all relationships,
letting go of our old grievances
and replacing them with new love.

Amen.

Light the large candle during the following Psalm.

Psalm

Psalm 119:105,113-114

Your word is a lamp for my feet,
A light on my path.
I hate a divided heart,
I love your Law.
You are my refuge and shield,
I put my hope in your word.

Trans. The New Jerusalem Bible

the undivided heart

Reading

Ezekiel 11:19-20a

I will give them a single heart and I will put a new spirit in them; I will remove the heart of stone from their bodies and give them a heart of flesh instead.

Trans. The Jerusalem Bible

Song

Restless Heart

I offer you my restless heart,
seeking undivided love.

© Trisha Watts 2002

Silence

Invite the participants to reflect quietly.

Reflection

Nelson Mandela

True reconciliation does not consist in merely forgetting the past.

Susan Ratcliffe & Helen Rappaport eds. The Little Oxford Dictionary of Quotations, Second Edition. (New York: Oxford University Press, 2001), 134.

Community Prayers

Invite the participants to each take a stone, symbolising their worries or burdens, from the pile at the base of the heart. Then, as the community prayers are said, ask them to each place their stone near the large candle.

Leader: Ever-present God, our hearts are divided when we think of people as 'us' and 'them'. May we appreciate life's diversities and work to build a common ground of respect between all peoples.

Hear our prayer, O God.

Response (sung): Listen and see with your heart. (From the song, Rest and Wait.)

Leader: Ever-present God, our hearts are divided when we are torn between the expectations of work and family. Help us remember that you are always with us in the everyday stuff of life, loving and supporting us.

Hear our prayer, O God.

Response.

Invite the participants to offer their own prayers to God, based on the above examples. When all have been offered, gather the prayers of the group by saying the following prayer.

Leader: Loving God, we bring these concerns before you, knowing that your heart is ready to receive us just as we are and to offer us healing.

Amen.

Song

Into Your Hands

Into your hands we place our burdens,
into your hands we place our trust,
knowing your hands are filled with mercy,
touching, restoring life.

© Trisha Watts 2002

Closing Prayer

Leader:

Spirit of compassion,
be the common ground on which we walk.
Be the common heart from which we talk.
Be the common breath that heals, restores and blesses us as
we go.

Amen.

healing grace

Introduction

Many times in our lives, we need to be assured of God's healing grace. In times of stress, illness, injury, despair and division, we need God's healing touch to mend our bodies and minds, our relationships and circumstances, our hearts and souls. When recovery seems impossible or life seems unbearable, we can always take comfort in God's soothing peace. This prayer time offers us the opportunity to release our bottled turmoil, anxiety and pain, and ask God to gently restore us to health, prosperity and unity.

Setting the Space

Firstly, arrange the lengths of fabric throughout the space, using boxes to attain different levels. Then, place the tea lights and vaporisers on the fabric and light them. Position the large candle in the centre of the space, and the bowls of oil on the floor at the front. Finally, arrange some green foliage or pot plants around the boxes.

Resources

- lengths of rainbow-coloured fabric
- several boxes
- tea lights
- two or three aromatherapy vaporisers with a fragrant healing oil, such as lavender, sandalwood, frankincense, tea-tree, eucalypt or boronia
- large candle
- fragrant oils for anointing, placed in two small bowls
- green foliage and/or pot plants
- CD player and instrumental music

healing grace

Welcome

When the participants are ready, offer them a warm greeting. Then, introduce the theme and practise the songs for the prayer time.

Invocation for the Land and its First People

Pause for a moment of silence.

Opening Prayer

> *Leader:*
>
> Author of life,
> why do I find my body and my life
> so often crippled with disease?
>
> I know that you intended me
> for completeness and well being.
>
> In your presence,
> it is clear that my feelings plant and nourish
> the seeds of disorder within me.
> I begin to see that my fears,
> anxieties and disappointments
> poison my relationships
> and peace of mind,
> leaving me vulnerable to illness.
>
> At other times,
> things do not seem so clear.
> I find myself clinging
> to what keeps me from wholeness,
> because the alternative
> seems too frightening or foreign.
> Your answers may be hard to accept
> because they seem too simple.

God of all light,
I ask for courage
to take steps towards healing,
even when they seem impossible.
Grant me patience
to listen to my body
when it tells me I have expected more
than I am able to do.
Help me to work with you
when I am standing in my own way.

Amen.

© Juliet Greentree 2003

Psalm

Psalm 103:1,3-5

Bless God, O my soul,
and all that is within me, bless God's holy name.
Bless God, O my soul
and do not forget all God's benefits –
who forgives all your iniquity,
who heals all your diseases,
who redeems your life from the pit,
who crowns you with steadfast love and mercy,
who satisfies you with good as long as you live,
so that your youth is renewed like the eagle's.

Trans. The New Century Psalter © 1999, The Pilgrim Press.

Reading

Luke 18:35-38,40-42

As he drew near to Jericho there was a blind man sitting at the side of the road begging. When he heard a crowd going past he asked what it was all about, and they told him that Jesus the Nazarene was passing by. So he called out, "Jesus, son of David, have pity on me."

Jesus stopped and ordered them to bring the man to him, and when he came up, asked him, "What do you want me to do for you?" "Sir", he replied, "let me see again." Jesus said to him, "Receive your sight. Your faith has saved you."

Trans. The New Jerusalem Bible

Song

Heal Me

I will live for you alone;
for you alone I'll live.
Heal me, heal me,
heal me and let me live.

© Trisha Watts 1994

Silence

Invite the participants to reflect quietly.

Community Prayers

Leader: Loving God, we ask for healing in our family relationships. May we learn to love without conditions and accept each person's differences.

Hear our prayer, O God.

Response (sung): Heal me and let me live. (From the song, Heal Me.)

Leader: Loving God, we ask for healing in our past relationships. May we release any anxiety or hurt associated with these memories.

Hear our prayer, O God.

Response.

Leader: Loving God, we ask for healing in our work relationships. May we find ways to practise respect and generosity of heart.

Hear our prayer, O God.

Response.

Invite the participants to offer their own prayers to God, ending each with the above response. Then, conclude the community prayers by saying the following prayer.

Leader: Great healing Spirit, we thank you for your tender love. Receive our hearts just as they are, and restore us to well being.

Through the light of Christ,

Amen.

Healing Blessing

Lift up the two bowls of oil during the following prayer.

Leader: Gracious God, bless this oil with the power of your Spirit to heal, renew and restore our lives.

Amen.

healing grace

Invite the participants to receive a healing blessing. Ask two assistants to hold the bowls of healing oil and anoint those who come forward by saying, "May you receive the Spirit's grace and healing". Play some quiet instrumental music during this time.

Song

Liberating Grace

> 1. Let us rise with you in liberating grace,
> with lives that know the power of your gaze.
>
> 2. Let us rise with you in liberating grace,
> with lives that know the freedom in your gaze.
>
> 3. Let us rise with you in liberating grace,
> with lives that know the healing in your gaze.

© Trisha Watts 1997

Closing Prayer

> *Leader:*
>
> God of Life,
> you pour through us, under us,
> over us and around us.
> Your power moves and touches us,
> graces us and heals us.
>
> Give us awareness and openness
> to welcome your healing light,
> your Holy Spirit,
> into our minds, our hearts,
> our lives and our world.
>
> Amen.

dreams and visions

Introduction

Dreams and visions are the daring desires of imagination. They are the passages between hope and reality, revealing to us the secrets of difference and change. In the frantic busyness of our lives, we need to take time to allow our minds to wander, to let our imaginations illuminate the deep longings of our souls. We need time to think about the future, to give shape, direction and purpose to our existence as God's people. This prayer time offers us the opportunity to reflect on the ways we may realise God's vision for us, and be inspired to make a difference in our lives and the lives of others.

Setting the Space

Place the box in the centre of the space and cover it with the length of gold fabric. Then, place the image of the transfiguration of Jesus on top of the box. Position the large candle in front of the box, with several tea lights surrounding it. Arrange the strips of coloured fabric in the basket, and position it with the coffee table and fabric markers on one side of the box. Place the hatstand or clothes horse on the other side.

Resources

- box
- length of gold fabric
- image of the transfiguration of Jesus
- large candle
- tea lights
- strips of coloured fabric for each participant, approximately 10 x 100 cm
- basket
- coffee table
- twelve fabric markers
- hatstand or clothes horse
- CD player and instrumental music

Welcome

When the participants are ready, offer them a warm greeting. Then, introduce the theme and practise the songs for the prayer time.

Invocation for the Land and its First People

Pause for a moment of silence.

Opening Prayer

> ### Leader:
>
> All-seeing God,
> at the gateway of this new beginning,
> we have come together
> to name not just everyday hopes and needs,
> but the essential yearnings
> which come from that best place in us,
> our eternal selves,
> abiding always in your presence.
>
> The flame of inspiration shines differently
> within each of our hearts,
> but as we move forward,
> unique yet together,
> our lights combine to illuminate the world around us
> with myriad colours.
>
> May your Spirit always walk in our midst,
> the light which is every perfection
> and all mysteries together.
>
> Amen.

Song

Walk in our Midst

> Walk in our midst, sacred light;
> source of hope, burning bright.

© Trisha Watts 2003

Reading

Matthew 17:1-2,5-8

> Jesus took with him Peter and James and his brother John and led them up a high mountain by themselves. There in their presence he was transfigured: his face shone like the sun and his clothes became as dazzling as light.
>
> Suddenly a bright cloud covered them with shadow, and suddenly from the cloud there came a voice which said, "This is my Son, the Beloved; he enjoys my favour. Listen to him." When they heard this, the disciples fell on their faces, overcome with fear. But Jesus came up and touched them, saying, "Stand up, do not be afraid." And when they raised their eyes they saw no one but Jesus.

Trans. The New Jerusalem Bible

Silence

Invite the participants to reflect quietly.

Reflection

Marianne Williamson

> Our deepest fear is not that we are inadequate. Our deepest fear is that we are powerful beyond measure. It is our

light, and not our darkness, that most frightens us. We ask ourselves, "Who am I to be brilliant, gorgeous, talented and fabulous?" Actually, who are you not to be? You are a child of God.

Your playing small doesn't serve the world. There's nothing enlightened about shrinking so that other people won't feel insecure around us. We were born to make manifest the glory of God within us. It's not just in some of us, it's in everyone. And as we let our own light shine, we unconsciously give other people permission to do the same. As we are liberated from our own fears, our presence automatically liberates others.

Marianne Williamson, A Return to Love. (Harper Collins Publishers, 1994)

Naming and Affirming Dreams and Visions

Invite the participants to come forward and write their dreams and visions for themselves and their world on the strips of fabric, using the fabric markers. As an example, the dreams and visions may be similar to the following:

- "I have a dream to make peace with those from whom I am distanced."

- "I have a dream that corporations will foster justice for all."

- "I have a dream that all religious beliefs will be respected."

- "I have a vision of love and respect for all children."

- "I have a vision of reconciliation with the land and its first people."

Once this activity is completed, ask the participants to drape the strips of fabric over the hatstand or clothes horse, creating a 'visioning tree'. Play some instrumental music during this time.

Invite participants to name their dreams and visions, affirming each with the communal response, "Empower us, O God".

> **Leader:** All-seeing, transfiguring God, you are the pulse behind the realisation of all good within this world. We ask that you hear the dreams and visions for ourselves and our world that we have named.

Reflections

An Australian Aboriginal Proverb

Those who lose dreaming are lost.

Julia Cameron, Walking in this World. (Penguin Putnam, Inc, 2002), 150

Malcolm Forbes

When you cease to dream, you cease to live.

M. Bryan, J. Cameron & C. Allen, The Artists' Way At Work. (Pan, 1998), 25

Community Prayers

> **Leader:** All-knowing God, we remember those who have lost their ability to dream and envision. Heal the wounds that disconnect them from their Source.

Hear us, we pray.

Response: Hear us, O God.

> **Leader:** We pray that we may find visioning companions on our way, people who are willing to create communities of hope that dare to dream what we hardly dared imagine.

Hear us, we pray.

Response.

Leader: We pray that we may be awake to the murmurings of the Spirit in the cries of the poor and oppressed.

Hear us, we pray.

Response.

Leader: We pray that world leaders initiate visionary policies which sustain and nourish society and creation.
Hear us, we pray.

Response.

Invite the participants to offer their own prayers for their lives and for the world. When all have been offered, gather the prayers of all present by saying the following prayer.

Leader: We gather these prayers in the knowledge that we are held and guided by your everlasting love.
Amen.

Song

Sacred Path

1. Let the glory of God shine bright
through eyes of compassion,
through hearts that believe.
Let the brilliance of God be light
for all those who seek a dream.

2. Let the glory of God shine out,
proclaiming creation with welcoming hearts,
liberating our fears and doubts.
We walk on a sacred path.

© Trisha Watts 2002

Closing Prayer

Leader:

Ever-present God,

May our eyes see the good in all Creation.
May our ears hear the music of harmonious relationships.
May our lips speak words of praise and affirmation.
May our hands offer kindness and blessing.
May our hearts carry God's dream of peace and justice for all.
May our feet walk on a sacred path, with Christ to guide our steps.

Amen.

sacred simplicity

Introduction

Living simply is not easy in the modern age. In every facet of our lives, matters seem to head onwards and upwards to complexity, with little we can do to stop them. The things we wear, the way we act, the words we say–everything we do can be carefully calculated to achieve an effect. But often our words are hollow and our actions meaningless. When we reflect, we see that all of this complexity, the mangled mess upon which we build our lives, is preventing us from truly connecting with God and the people we love. We need to return to the simplicity that Jesus preached, a divine simplicity out of which genuine love and care may grow. This prayer time offers us the opportunity to strip away all that is meaningless and worthless from our lives, so that we may present ourselves to God as we truly are.

> **Resources**
>
> - box
> - length of earth-coloured fabric
> - large candle
> - large basket of fresh flowers
> - tea lights
> - decorated 'talking stick'

Setting the Space

Cover the box with the length of earth-coloured fabric and place it in the centre of the space, with the large candle on top. Lean the basket against the base of the box, with the flowers spilling out. Arrange the tea lights around the flowers, and place the talking stick on the ground, to one side. Light the tea lights.

sacred simplicity

Welcome

When the participants are ready, offer them a warm greeting.
Then, introduce the theme and practice the songs for the prayer time.

Invocation for the Land and its First People

Light the large candle and pause for a moment of silence.

Opening Prayer

> *Leader:*
>
> Wondrous God,
> joy and simplicity,
> love and play
> are gifts you graciously give.
>
> May we have the courage
> to come into your presence,
> bringing our whole selves,
> looking for moments of joy,
> living simply and trustfully,
> and loving boldly and playfully.
>
> We are willing to let go.
> We seek liberation.
> We are ready.
>
> Amen.

Song

Deep Waters

Deep waters flowing,
calling all to follow.
Watching, listening, waiting;
silence finds a home.

© Trisha Watts 1992

Reading

Luke 12:22-26

Jesus said to his disciples:

"I tell you not to worry about your life! Don't worry about having something to eat or wear. Life is more than food or clothing. Look at the crows! They don't plant or harvest, and they don't have storehouses or barns. But God takes care of them. You are much more important than any birds. Can worry make you live longer? If you don't have power over small things, why worry about everything else?"

Trans. The Contemporary English Version

Silence

Invite the participants to reflect quietly.

Reflective Questions

Invite the participants to ponder the following questions.

- What does 'simplicity' mean?
- How can we create simplicity amongst the complexities of our lives?

- What is meant by the saying, "live simply so that others may simply live"?

- How can we resist entanglement in the complexities of other people's lives?

- Is living simply a sacred practice?

A 'talking stick' is a traditional prop used in story telling. Whoever holds the stick is given the authority to speak. Invite two or three participants to share their responses to the reflective questions using the talking stick.

Community Prayers

Leader: Loving Spirit, teach us the art of living simply. Help us to share the gifts of friendship, food, faith and freedom with all we meet.

Hear us, we pray.

Response (sung): You are a spring of water that never runs dry, that never runs dry. (From the song, Spring of Water.)

Leader: Loving Spirit, help us to slow down so that we may savour and delight in the treasures of each day.

Hear us, we pray.

Response.

Leader: Loving Spirit, encourage us to take time to develop spaciousness of body and mind, releasing the guilt and over-responsibility in our lives.

Hear us, we pray.

Response.

Leader: Loving Spirit, remind us to return to the basic simplicity of human life, that of mindful breathing, the source of all action.

Hear us, we pray.

Response.

Leader: Loving Spirit, help us to get out of our own way, and simply trust that all will be well.

Hear us, we pray.

Response.

Invite the participants to offer their own prayers to God, concluding each with the sung response. Then, conclude the community prayers by saying the following prayer.

Leader: O God, Jesus lived his life with radical simplicity, carrying only what was necessary for his journey. Take our hands and walk with us, so that we may be bold enough to reduce the clutter in our lives, living in faith and attending to only what is essential.

Amen.

Song

All Will Be Well

1a. Let your body sway with creation.

Chorus:

All will be well,
all will be well.

1b. Let your spirit sing with elation.

Chorus.

2a. Joining hands with sister and brother.

Chorus.

2b. Sharing peace with stranger and lover.

Chorus.

3a. Praising God with joy and gladness.

Chorus.

3b. Stepping out with love and goodness.

Chorus.

© Trisha Watts 2002

Closing Prayer

Leader:

God of Wonder,
the simplicity of sun on a window sill,
of ducks gliding on a pond,
of clouds piling up in a blue sky,
of a baby's laughter
is my request.

Please grace me with freedom.
Shine your light on me,
so that I may shine it out
on all I see.

Amen.

Invite the participants to take a flower from the basket as a symbol of living simply.

spring

Introduction

Spring is a time of regeneration and new hope. The bleak desolation of winter has passed, and we look forward to brighter days and warmer nights. As blossoms burst out across the earth, we are reminded that God has safely brought us through the darkness, and now opens our eyes to the brilliant light of God's love. Just like the seed planted in the damp winter soil, we are enlivened by the warm sunshine, and reach out with renewed vigour. This prayer time offers us the opportunity to welcome this new season with joy and gladness, thanking God for the gift of new life and the promise of happy days.

Resources

- several lengths of different earth-coloured fabrics
- vases of fresh flowers
- colourful fruit
- tea lights
- image of Christ
- large candle

Setting the Space

Arrange the lengths of fabric, flowers, fruit and tea lights as a focal point in the centre of the space. Place the image of Christ and the large candle in the very centre of this arrangement. Light all the candles except the large candle.

Welcome

When the participants are ready, offer them a warm greeting. Then, introduce the theme and practise the songs for the prayer time.

Invocation for the Land and its First People

Pause for a moment of silence.

Opening Prayer

> *Leader:*
>
> Springtime God,
> thank you for giving us one another
> and this holy place where we find you.
>
> We thank you for the newness
> of this season
> and all its hopes,
> spreading before us
> like a carpet of flowers.
>
> Let us live in the freshness
> of a new season
> with new life,
> new love
> and new work.
> Let your springtime
> touch our hearts and souls,
> so that everything we think, do and say
> spreads your ancient beauty ever new.
> Let our sad and tired hearts
> look ahead with new hope.
>
> Amen.

Song

Our Lives are Turning

Our lives are turning and changing view,
time for the old to give way to the new.

© Trisha Watts 2002

Light the large candle during the following reading.

Reading

Song of Songs 2:10-12

My love lifts up his voice,
he says to me,
"Come then, my beloved,
my lovely one, come.
For see, winter is passed,
the rains are over and gone.

Flowers are appearing on the earth.
The season of glad songs has come,
the cooing of the turtledove is heard in our land."

Trans. The New Jerusalem Bible

Song

Winter is Past

Chorus:

Winter is past,
the snows are over and gone.
Winter is past,
the flowers appear on the earth.

1. Come, my lovely one, come!
   See the blossoming vines.
   Hear the turtle doves
   cooing from the heights.

© Trisha Watts 2004

Silence

Invite the participants to reflect quietly.

Reading

Hosea 14:9

I am like an evergreen cypress,
you owe your fruitfulness to me.

Trans. The New Jerusalem Bible

Reading

Hildegard of Bingen

The air, with its penetrating strength, characterises the victorious banner that is trust. It gives light to the fire's flame and sprinkles the imagination of believers with the dew of hope. Thus does trust show the way. Those who breathe this dew long for heavenly things. They carry within a refreshing, fulfilling, greening love with which they hasten to the aid of all. With the passion of heavenly yearning, they produce rich fruit.

Gabriele Uhlein, Meditations with Hildegard of Bingen. (New Mexico: Bear & Company, 1983), 69

Community Prayers

Leader: Springtime God, we pray for the community gathered here. May each person find hope in this time of regeneration.

Hear us, we pray.

Response: Refresh and inspire us, O God.

Leader: For those who are rejoicing in a rich spring harvest. May they be prepared to share their wealth with those whose harvest has failed this year.

Hear us, we pray.

Response.

Leader: For our country and its leaders, legislators and public servants. May they remain open to new paths and exercise conscience and goodwill.

Hear us, we pray.

Response.

Leader: For our prophets, justice-criers, poets and artists who use the language of creativity to proclaim the messages of humanity.

Hear us, we pray.

Response.

Invite the participants to offer their joys or concerns to God. Once all have been offered, close the community prayers by saying the following prayer.

Leader: Greening God, our prayers rise to you like wafts of springtime perfume. May you receive them in generosity and love.

Amen.

Song

Spring is Here

Sing out loud, all the earth!
Spring is here, announcing birth!
Sing out loud, joyfully!
Blossoms dance abundantly!

© Trisha Watts 2004

Closing Prayer

Leader:

God of radiant life,
we give thanks to you.
Through times of faith without sight,
you have brought us safely
through the darkness
and sheltered us with gentle hands,
bringing us gently back into the light.

May the joy of blossoming flowers
be in our hands
and our everyday work.
May the glory of spring be in our eyes
and our perceiving.
May the colours, flowers,
stars, breezes,
golden days and glimmering nights,
and all other gifts of spring
fill our souls with gladness and peace.

Amen.

© Juliet Greentree 2004

summer

Introduction

Summer is a time to revel in the fruits of God's love. All around us, nature sings with content, basking in the high midday sun and the deep blue skies above. God's voice speaks to us in the singing of the birds, the crashing of the waves, the swaying of the trees and the ticking of the crickets. Life is fully alive! We are called by God to imitate the vitality and sparkle of life that surrounds us, challenging ourselves to reach out with renewed love, hope, happiness and faith. This prayer time offers us the opportunity to give thanks and praise to God for the blessings of summer, and be determined to savour every moment of this season of life.

> **Resources**
>
> - mosquito net
> - candles of varying sizes
> - sacred image
> - large candle
> - bowl of cherries
> - bowl of star jasmine, jacaranda or other scented summer flower

Setting the Space

Hang or drape the mosquito net as a backdrop. Arrange the candles on different levels throughout the space, or in a circle around the sacred image and the large candle. Place the bowl of cherries near the image, and the bowl of summer flowers near the entrance to the room. As the participants arrive, invite them to take a flower from the bowl. Light all candles except the large candle.

Welcome

When the participants are ready, offer them a warm greeting.
Then, introduce the theme and practise the songs for the prayer time.

Invocation for the Land and its First People

Pause for a moment of silence.

Opening Prayer

> ### Leader:
>
> Renewing God,
> it is now the time
> when morning comes early
> and twilight lingers long.
> The days are bright,
> as the heat slips from the sun over our skin.
> The sky is blue and deep as dreams.
>
> This is a time for opening.
> New plans, new friendships take shape
> in the gentle womb of the jasmine night.
> In our sleep, our blood sings
> with the song of the joyful earth.
>
> Ah, our Maker,
> we change and grow old,
> but your summer perpetually renews us
> with the youth of hope.
> We bless you for your providence.
>
> Amen.

© Juliet Greentree 2004

Canticle of Thanksgiving

Leader: We give thanks and praise for the blessings of summer.

For its colour, sunshine, refreshing waters and blue skies.

Response (sung): We give thanks, we give thanks, we give thanks. (From the song, We Give Thanks.)

Leader: For long hours of daylight and sparkling night skies.

Response.

Leader: For outdoor activities, where friends and family can gather under the shade of trees, umbrellas and marquees.

Response.

Leader: For beaches, pools, creeks and waterholes, the places where we can cool off and have fun.

Response.

Invite the participants to each offer a prayer of thanksgiving as they place their flowers beside the sacred image. Once all prayers have been offered, light the large candle.

Reading

Isaiah 44:3-4

I shall pour out water on the thirsty soil
and streams on the dry ground.
I shall pour out my spirit on your descendants,
my blessing on your offspring,
and they will spring up among the grass,
like willows on the banks of a stream.

Trans. The New Jerusalem Bible

Song

Like a Tree

> Like a tree that stands by the stream,
> send deep your roots to the water.
> Be not afraid of the weather that comes;
> you will bear fruit if you trust in my love.

© Trisha Watts 1993

Silence

Invite the participants to reflect quietly.

Community Prayers

Leader: Gracious God, as we gather in this circle of faith, we remember those who need strength and encouragement.

For the sick, the lonely, the lost and the vulnerable. May the gifts of summer time give them hope, we pray.

Response (sung): You will bear fruit if you trust in my love. (From the song, *Like A Tree.*)

Leader: For the tired and weary, who are thirsting for spiritual, physical and emotional support, we pray.

Response.

Leader: For those living in the midst of drought and famine, where another hot day promises only dust and despair, we pray.

Response.

Invite the participants to offer prayers for their families, communities and the world. Once all have been offered, gather the prayers of the group together by saying the following prayer.

Leader: Expansive God, hear the prayers of our hearts this day. May we step out with boldness, confident in your presence and loving providence.

Amen.

Song

All Will Be Well

1a. Let your body sway with creation.

Chorus:

All will be well,
all will be well.

1b. Let your spirit sing with elation.

Chorus.

2a. Joining hands with sister and brother.

Chorus.

2b. Sharing peace with stranger and lover.

Chorus.

3a. Praising God with joy and gladness.

Chorus.

3b. Stepping out with love and goodness.

Chorus.

© Trisha Watts 2002

Closing Prayer

Leader:

God of summer,
of morning sun at five o'clock,
of evening light at nine,
of dark cherries in bowls,
and long, cold drinks.

God of long hot days and sultry nights,
bless us with sudden thunderstorms.
Protect us from the hailstones
and remind us to cover up
in the heat of the sun.

Provide us with the deep peace
of your green shade.
Spread your tablecloth on the grass before us,
tempting us with your loving understanding,
acceptance, trust,
joy and sweet simplicity.

Indulge us as we build our castles in the sand,
and when the waves wash them away,
please dry our tears.

Remind us that at the end of the day,
we all come home to you.

Amen.

autumn/fall

Introduction

Autumn (Fall) is a time of preparation and change. It reminds us that in the midst of life, we must ready ourselves for times of hardship and loss, even death. The abundance of summer has passed, and the harshness of winter beckons. We must gather the fruits of sunshine and harvest, and place them in safe keeping for the future. This prayer time offers us the opportunity to draw ourselves closer to God, allowing God's infinite love and goodness to protect us from the cold and comfort us in our loss.

Setting the Space

Make a decorative arrangement using the fabric, grapes, dried leaves, dry branches, tea lights and small candles. Place the items on a variety of levels, with the large candle as a focal point in the centre. Light all candles except the large candle.

Resources

- lengths of brown, red and ochre fabric
- bunches of grapes
- large quantity of dried leaves
- dry branches
- tea lights
- small candles
- large candle

Welcome

When the participants are ready, offer them a warm greeting.
Then, introduce the theme and practise the songs for the prayer time.

Invocation for the Land and its First People

Pause for a moment of silence.

Opening Prayer

> ### Leader:
>
> Wondrous God,
> the leaves are falling around us
> through days growing
> ever clearer and more barren.
> Surrounded by little deaths,
> the drying of the grass
> and shrivelling of the flowers,
> we gather our lives in
> like the harvest.
>
> Our friendships,
> our experiences,
> our achievements
> we wrap around ourselves,
> against the coldness which is to come.
> For in this time,
> our lives will be lived within.
>
> Like the grapes that are harvested
> in happy sunlight,
> turning to wine in dark cellars,
> our thoughts will transform
> and grow richer.

Come, Spirit of all mysteries,
into the centre of our containment.
Grow treasure from within us.
This we pray.

© Juliet Greentree 2004

Light the large candle during the following song.

Song

A Time for Every Season

Chorus:

There is a time for ev'ry season under heaven.
There is a time for ev'ry season under heaven.

1. A time for birthing, a time for dying;
   a time for uprooting, a time to plant;
   a time for killing, a time for healing;
   a time for ev'rything.

Chorus.

2.   A time for weeping, a time for laughing;
   a time for mourning, a time to dance;
   a time for searching, a time for losing;
   a time for ev'rything.

Chorus.

3. A time for tearing, a time for mending;
   a time for silence, a time to speak;
   a time for loving, a time for hating;
   a time for ev'rything.

Chorus.

© Trisha Watts 2002

Psalm

Psalm 51:10-12

God, create a clean heart in me,
put into me a new and constant spirit,
do not banish me from your presence,
do not deprive me of your holy spirit.

Be my saviour again, renew my joy,
keep my spirit steady and willing.

Trans. The Jerusalem Bible

Reading

Wu-men (1183-1260)

Ten thousand flowers in spring, the moon in autumn,
a cool breeze in summer, snow in winter.
If your mind isn't clouded by unnecessary things,
this is the best season of your life.

Stephen Mitchell, The Enlightened Heart. (USA: Harper Perennial, 1993) 47

Song

Our Lives are Turning

Our lives are turning and changing view;
time for the old to give way to the new.

© Trisha Watts 2002

Silence

Invite the participants to reflect quietly.

Community Prayers

Leader: Loving God, in this autumn (fall) season, as the leaves turn to gold and rust, may our hearts and eyes turn to the concerns of our changing world.

For those who are experiencing unemployment, the loss of a loved one, disease in body, or exile from family or home, we pray.

Response: Compassionate God, hear us.

Leader: For those who are facing the autumn years of their lives, aware of the magnificence and fragility of human life, we pray.

Response.

Leader: For those who are thinking ahead, planning and consolidating with untiring love, we pray.

Response.

Invite the participants to offer their own prayers to God, concluding each with the above response. Then, conclude the community prayers by saying the following prayer.

Leader: Loving God, as the daylight fades and we need more protection and warmth, we thank you for your unconditional love. Receive our heartfelt prayers this day.

Amen.

Song

Clear as Day

> In the darkness, you are light,
> shining clearly, ever bright.
> To you the darkness is not dark,
> and the night is clear as day.

© Trisha Watts 2003

Closing Prayer

Leader:

May all that is not love fall away.
May all that is not truth fall away.
May all that is not fullness fall away.
May all that is not richness fall away.
May all that is not peaceful fall away.
May this autumn (fall) season's soft release
bring us closer to your all-embracing love.

Through and with the love of Christ,

Amen.

winter

Introduction

Winter is a time of turning inwards. As temperatures drop and the earth turns barren, we need to seek warmth and sustenance in the shelter of God's love. Through days growing ever shorter, we can take time to reflect on our lives. All our deadness and dryness must be cut away, so that we may begin anew when the sunshine of spring ushers new life through the surface. This prayer time offers us the opportunity to rediscover direction and purpose, and ask God to carry us safely through the darkness.

Setting the Space

Place the length of dark fabric on the floor, with the large candle in the centre. Arrange all other items around the candle. Light all candles except the large candle.

Resources

- length of dark fabric
- large candle
- pruning shears
- dead branches
- large bowl, filled with earth
- tea lights
- sacred image
- flower bulbs, such as tulips or daffodils (optional)

Welcome

When the participants are ready, offer them a warm greeting.
Then, introduce the theme and practise the songs for the prayer time.

Invocation for the Land and its First People

Pause for a moment of silence.

Song

Love the Winter

> Love the winter,
> when the plant says nothing.

© Trisha Watts 1999

Opening Prayer

Leader:

Winter,
a time of snow and wetness.
The days are short and cold,
the deciduous trees are bare.

Winter,
a time for cutting away
dead wood from roses,
and pruning unwanted branches
from grape vines.

Winter,
a time of shaping things
and tying up the waste.

Winter,
a time for clearing,
cool and passionless.

Yet, in this time,
there is still growth:
the flower withers
to form the seedcase,
just as souls need to be empty
before they can be filled to overflowing.

Under the earth,
tubers shrink and turn inside out,
sending up the shafts of stem
and sending down the anchoring roots.

Underneath everything,
in the darkness,
new life is seething,
yearning to break through the surface.

The husks fall away from the seed
and the ticking kernel starts to shoot.

Song

Let Your Roots Sink Deep

Let your roots sink deep;
anchor in abiding love.

© Trisha Watts 2002

Reading

John 12:24-25

I tell you for certain that a grain of wheat that falls on the
ground will never be more than one grain unless it dies. But if

it dies, it will produce lots of wheat. If you love your life, you will lose it. If you give it up in this world, you will be given eternal life.

Trans. The Contemporary English Version

Song

Surrender to the Earth

Like a grain of wheat,
surrender to the earth;
resting, yielding, emptying.

© Trisha Watts 2003

Silence

Invite the participants to reflect quietly.

Community Prayers

Leader: Warming God, we remember the cycles of life and the time of winter. They invite us to turn inwards and reflect on the choices in our lives. (Pause.)

We remember our families, partners, children, loved ones and work mates. May the seeds of new life receive nourishment from the soils of love and care.

For this, we pray.

Response: Hear our prayer.

Leader: We remember those who find winter a time of loneliness and coldness through lack of companionship. May we be willing to share the warmth of friendship and care with them.

For this, we pray.

Response.

Leader: We pray for those who live on the streets of our cities and towns. May their immediate need for shelter and protection be met.

For this, we pray.

Response.

Leader: We pray for those who feel exiled through shame or guilt, torn from the warm hearths of family and community. May we extend arms of openness and acceptance to them.

For this, we pray.

Response.

Leader: We pray for our world. As we experience the depths of winter, half of the planet is living in the heat of summer. May we remember with wonder the balancing of the earth's resources and our interconnection with one another. Let us not lose sight of the bigger picture amidst our everyday joys and struggles.

For this, we pray.

Response.

Invite the participants to offer a their own prayers to God, ending each with the above response. Then, conclude the community prayers by saying the following prayer.

Leader: God of all seasons, we place our concerns, spoken and unspoken, into your loving hands. We know that you are the source of faithful love.

Amen.

Invite the participants to each take a flower bulb as a symbol of the planting of new life during winter.

Song

Seeds Planted

> Seeds planted deep in the Ground of Being,
> leaning, growing towards the light.

© Trisha Watts 2003

Closing Prayer

> ### Leader:
>
> Loving Spirit,
> like the gentle sun in winter,
> you penetrate the darkness within,
> enlivening,
> quickening,
> invigorating us.
>
> You shine away our deadness,
> our numbness.
> Your Spirit ignites us,
> until we slowly realise
> that our winter has thawed,
> and we are warm and loving.
>
> Bless us,
> the seeds in your ground.
>
> Amen.

thanksgiving

Introduction

God's generosity is truly limitless. Everywhere we look, we can witness the countless blessings God has given us. From the twinkling stars to the rich brown earth, from the spontaneous smile to the spring in someone's step, from the soaring of an eagle to the creeping of a mouse, from the sound of hearty laughter to the smell of sweet perfume, the grace of God strikes all our senses. This prayer time offers us the opportunity to appreciate the many gifts that God has given us, and to offer our grateful hearts to God in thanks and praise.

Setting the Space

Place the cardboard boxes at a variety of different levels, and arrange the lengths of yellow fabric over them. Then, position the tea lights randomly on the boxes, with the large candle in the centre. Place the large pottery bowl filled with incense sticks on the floor, in front of the large candle. Finally, arrange a number of pot plants around the setting.

Resources

- several cardboard boxes
- several lengths of yellow fabric
- tea lights
- large candle
- large ceramic bowl or dish, filled with incense sticks
- pot plants

Welcome

When the participants are ready, offer them a warm greeting.
Then, introduce the theme and practise the songs for the prayer time.

Invocation for the Land and its First People

Pause for a moment of silence.

Opening Prayer

Leader:

We give thanks for this time of gathering,
a time for reflection on all the good things that fill our lives:
friends, families, communities, the love of children.

There is so much we take for granted.
Your riches surround us like the air we breathe
and we fail to notice them.

In this world of separation, it is good to gather like this,
bound by a love that frees our full potential.
Let us give thanks for this.

Amen.

Song

Spring of Water

You are a spring of water
that never runs dry,
that never runs dry.

© Trisha Watts 1992

Prayers of Thanksgiving

Light the large candle and an incense stick.

> *Leader:* For the freedom to gather as a community seeking God.

> *Response:* We give thanks with grateful hearts.

> *Leader:* For the mysteries of the world in which we live.

> *Response.*

> *Leader:* For the comfort and support of our families and loved ones.

> *Response.*

Invite the participants to offer their own prayers of thanksgiving. When all have been offered, say the following prayer.

> *Leader:* Loving God, may these prayers of thanksgiving rise from our hearts like fragrant incense.

> Amen.

Psalm

Psalm 147:1-3,7

> Shout praises to the Lord! Our God is kind,
> and it is right and good to sing praises to God.
> The Lord rebuilds Jerusalem
> and brings the people of Israel back home again.
> God renews our hopes and heals our bodies.

> Celebrate and sing!
> Play your harps for the Lord our God.

Trans. The Contemporary English Version

thanksgiving

Reading

Philippians 1:3-4

I thank my God whenever I think of you, and every time I pray for you all, I always pray with joy.

Trans. The New Jerusalem Bible

Silence

Invite the participants to reflect quietly.

Community Prayers

Leader: Loving God, we take time now to remember our families, communities and world. We pray for those who are unable to give thanks for this day because of heavy–heartedness.

Response: Comforting Spirit, hear us.

Leader: We pray for those who are denied the basic human rights of security, dignity and respect.

Response.

Leader: We pray for those who are voiceless in our society.

Response.

Leader: We pray for those who forge new pathways to justice and freedom.

Response.

Leader: We pray for those who nurture and affirm the gift of life.

Response.

Invite the participants to offer their own prayers to God, ending each with the above response. Then, conclude the community prayers by saying the following prayer.

Leader: We pray for all the joys and concerns in our hearts today, spoken and unspoken. Comforting Spirit, hear our humble prayers.

Response: Amen.

Pass the bowl of incense sticks around the group. Invite each participant to take an incense stick as a symbol of their continuing prayers of thanksgiving.

Closing Prayer

Leader:

Our Parent,
we thank you for our bodies.
We thank you for shelter and food.
We thank you for the world
which is our home,
with its forests and deserts and oceans.
We thank you for the unexpected treasures
which enrich our lives,
for the starry night sky
and the dog's wagging tail.
We thank you for the mysteries
of love and relationships.
We thank you for songs, stories,
dancing and laughter.

You have given us this wealth,
and we are humbled by it.

Thank you, gracious God, for life!

© Juliet Greentree 2004

Song

We Give Thanks

We give thanks for the goodness of love that is shared.
We give thanks for this circle around which we are fed.
We give thanks for the beauty of friends and family.
We give thanks, we give thanks, we give thanks.

We give thanks for tomorrow and thanks for today
We give thanks for the journey and faith along the way.
We give thanks for the promise of Jesus with us now.
We give thanks, we give thanks, we give thanks.

© Trisha Watts and Monica O'Brien 2002

honouring our ancestors

Introduction

Our ancestors lay the foundations for our identity. In passing on their culture, race and religious beliefs, they provide us with a sense of who we are and where we belong. We have inherited the blessings of their toil and faith, just as we will pass on the fruits of our lives to those who come after us. We, like them, can choose life for ourselves and for future generations. This prayer time offers us the opportunity to honour the memory of our ancestors and recognise their continued influence on our lives.

Setting the Space

Hang the length of dark fabric as a backdrop. Create a small alcove with the bricks or concrete blocks, and place the tea lights inside, with the large candle and the symbol of the trinity in the centre. Position the three coloured candles in front of the large candle. Place the sandbox in front of the alcove, and the basket of small candles and the 'talking stick' to one side.

> **Resources**
>
> - length of dark fabric
> - ten bricks or concrete blocks
> - tea lights
> - large candle
> - symbol of the trinity
> - sandbox
> - three coloured candles
> - small candles, placed in a basket
> - decorated 'talking stick'

Welcome

When the participants are ready, offer them a warm greeting.
Then, introduce the theme and practise the songs for the prayer time.

Invocation for the Land and its First People

Pause for a moment of silence.

Opening Prayer

Leader:

Ever-present God,
let us honour our ancestors,
our mothers and fathers
stretching back in time
to distant lands and different tongues.

Their songs and stories,
their loves and fears
were passed down to us,
time out of mind.

In us, the past is gathered up
and the future opens up.
Let us honour those who went before.

We bless them with our love.
They never knew us, but we know of them.
They kept life moving,
kept love flowering.
Their blood and spirit flows in us,
unfolding generations yet unborn.

Bless them, our ancestors,
and may they bless us too.

Honouring our Ancestors

Light the first coloured candle.

> **Leader:** We light this candle in honour of our ancestors, the bedrock of our lives. We place their names before God.

Light the second coloured candle.

> **Leader:** We light this candle in honour of those whose courageous love, even in the face of death, gave hope to the oppressed. We place their names before God.

Light the third coloured candle.

> **Leader:** We light this candle in honour of those whose teachings have continued throughout time to inspire compassion, wisdom and justice. We place their names before God.

Remembrance of our Ancestors

A 'talking stick' is a traditional prop used in story telling. Whoever holds the stick is given the authority to speak. Invite the participants to share a story of their ancestry using the talking stick.

Reading

Deuteronomy 30:19

I set before you life or death, blessing or curse. Choose life, then, so that you and your descendants may live.

Trans. The Jerusalem Bible

Song

Choose Life

> Choose life,
> that you and your children may live, may live.
> Choose life,
> that you and your children may live.
>
> I set before you life or death.
> I set before you blessing and choice.
>
> Choose life,
> that you and your children may live.
>
> © Trisha Watts 2002

Silence

Invite the participants to reflect quietly.

Community Prayers

During this prayer, take a candle from the basket, light it from the large candle and place it in the sandbox.

> **Leader:** We light this candle in remembrance of the needs of our families. We place them into your hands, O God.
>
> **Response:** Hear our prayer.
>
> **Leader:** We light this candle in remembrance of our friends who are struggling with illness and change. We place them into your hands, O God.
>
> **Response.**

honouring our ancestors

Leader: We light this candle in remembrance of the tensions of our world. We place them into your hands, O God.

Response.

Invite the participants to come forward and each take a candle from the basket. Then, ask them to light their candles from the large candle, and place them in the sandbox. Encourage them to offer their own prayers to God. Conclude the community prayers by saying the following prayer.

Leader: Light of Christ, we give thanks for those who nurture the flame of faith. May we receive the blessings of our faith inheritance, and have the courage to share these blessings with those who are to come.

Amen.

Song

Source of Being

We all return to the source of being,
each and every one.
We all return to the source of loving
when our time has come.

© Trisha Watts 2003

Closing Prayer

All:

Source of All,
we give thanks for the tribes we came from
and for our individual family streams,
the generations of the past
whose strengths and challenges inspire us today.

Give us courage to speak out our truths.
Give us openness when we communicate with those
who have a different story from ours.

Be with us on our journey,
as we move towards you,
our Origin.

Amen.

blessed are the women

Introduction

Women have unique gifts. Whether in their families or their communities, they bring a refreshing vibrancy, resolve, compassion and charity to the challenges of everyday life. As both mother and daughter, sister and aunt, godmother and grandmother, companion and friend they constantly nurture the gift of life, joyfully accepting the great responsibility that has been placed in their hands. This prayer time offers us the opportunity to acknowledge, affirm and celebrate the special gifts of women.

Setting the Space

Place the candelabrum in the centre of the space, with the green foliage around it. Then, place the stool and shawl on one side of the candelabrum, and arrange the bowls of lavender and bookmarks around the base of the stool.

Resources

- four large candles on a four-branched cande-labrum
- green foliage
- stool
- shawl
- bowl of lavender sprigs
- bowl of bookmarks printed with 'A Life-Giving Creed' (see below)

blessed are the women

Welcome

When the participants are ready, offer them a warm greeting.
Then, introduce the theme and practise the songs for the prayer time.

Light the first candle on the candelabrum, and pause for a moment
of silence.

Invocation for the Land and its First People

Pause for a moment of silence.

Invocation for Women

Light the second candle on the candelabrum, and pray the following prayer.

> ***Leader:*** We light this candle in honour of our grandmothers
> and ancestors, the wellsprings of our history.

> ***Response:*** May they be blessed.

Light the third candle on the candelabrum, and pray the following prayer.

> ***Leader:*** We light this candle in honour of our birth mothers,
> who laboured to give us life.

> ***Response.***

Light the fourth candle on the candelabrum, and pray the following prayer.

> ***Leader:*** We light this candle in honour of our adoptive and
> spiritual mothers, who have midwived the births of our spir-
> itual and physical endeavours.

> ***Response.***

Opening Prayer

Leader:

We come together and welcome one another.
The same deep longing brings us here,
our human longing to be heard, to be seen,
to be treated with dignity and respect.

Too many voices go unheard,
and we must speak for them:
love compels us because we are part of them.
It is the world's longing
and we voice it for all people.

Loving God,
help us end the restless search for our strength
and reveal to each of us the truth of where it lies:
deep within our large and loving hearts and minds.

Our cathedral is the world,
our congregation everyone we meet
or think about or touch.

The message that we bring
is one of celebration,
of joyful inclusion without exception.

Amen.

Song

I Have Loved You

I have loved you with an everlasting love.
I am constant in my affection for you.

© Trisha Watts 2003

Psalm

Psalm 139:13-15

It was you who created my inmost self,
and put me together in my mother's womb;
for all these mysteries I thank you;
for the wonder of myself,
for the wonder of your works.

You know me through and through,
from having watched my bones take shape
when I was being formed in secret,
knitted together in the limbo of the womb.

Trans. The Jerusalem Bible

Reading

Wisdom 6:12-14

Wisdom is bright, and does not grow dim.
By those who love her, she is readily seen,
and found by those who look for her.
Quick to anticipate those who desire her,
she makes herself known to them.
Watch for her early and you will have no trouble;
you will find her sitting at your gates.

Trans. The Jerusalem Bible

Silence

Pause for a moment of silence.

Sharing Our Stories

Invite the participants to reflect on the wisdom, knowledge and guidance they have gained through the interaction with women in their lives. Then, invite two or three participants to place the shawl on their shoulders in turn, and each share their reflection with the group.

Community Prayers

Leader: Loving God, we remember the women in our lives who have shaped and gifted us with their nurturing, affirmation, courage and enthusiasm.

Response: Encircle them, we pray.

Leader: We remember the women whose intuitive hearts acknowledge the divine in their daily rituals. Guide them in their awareness of the sacred in the ordinary.

Response.

Leader: We remember the women who are in the midst of change in their personal and family relationships, whether through separation, divorce or loss. Help them to deal with their grief and the challenges of a new way of life.

Response.

Leader: We remember the women who are raising children by themselves, struggling with the every day task of making and maintaining a nurturing home.

Response.

Leader: We remember the places in our world where women and their rights are not respected.

Response:

Leader: We remember the women who juggle a career and family responsibilities. May they always find breathing space and support in their lives.

Response.

Leader: We remember the contributions women have made to all areas of life: their ability to lead or follow, their intuition and emotional intelligence in the work place, and their sensuality, playfulness and empathy in communities.

Response.

Invite the participants to offer their own prayers for women, ending each with the above response. Then, conclude the community prayers by saying the following prayer.

Leader: Gracious God, we ask you to gather all our prayers, spoken and unspoken, to your loving heart.

Amen.

Passing On of Peace

Pass the bowls of lavender and bookmarks around the group. Invite each participant to take a sprig of lavender and bookmark containing 'A Life-Giving Creed' as a sign of peace.

A Life-Giving Creed

All:

I give myself permission to stand still and breathe!

I believe in the gifts and beauty of all people: women, men and children.

I believe in the gift of myself.

I give freely to others and receive with grace.

I laugh with others and to myself.

I support and protect others and know my own limits.

I am a master juggler and choose to take time to reflect.

I am open and yet can keep confidences.

I am willing to shed tears of joy and weep tears of sorrow.

I am a strong anchor and can fly like an eagle.

Song

Women of the World

> Sisters, we the midwives,
> women of the world, strong, alive!
> Sacred is the path we tread,
> blessings we will spread.

© Trisha Watts 2003

Closing Prayer

Leader:

Loving Spirit,
we ask you for these gifts:
goals without ruthlessness,
self-esteem without self-righteousness,
community without neglect,
a place to remain soft when life is hard,
joy and confidence,
passion and well being.

Amen.

refugees

Introduction

Refuge is one of the most basic human needs. No one should be denied the feelings of safety, comfort and security that come with having a place to call home. However, in our world of privileges and luxuries, where shelter and hospitality come so freely, it is easy to forget their value. We are blessed with a freedom and bounty that many people cannot even imagine. We live without the daily fear of persecution, intimidation, violence, isolation and death. The refugees of this world are people cast away by their own countries, severed from family and friends, and left floating in a sea of uncertainty. Jesus reminds us to openly welcome the stranger into our land, offering healing with actions of love and care. This prayer time offers us an opportunity to pray for those who are desperately seeking refuge, and awaken ourselves to hear their calls for help.

Resources

- box
- length of black fabric
- large sand tray or planter box, filled with soil
- basket of taper candles
- large candle
- hoop of barbed wire
- tea lights
- multi-lingual welcome sign (e.g. 'bienvenue', 'wellkommen') or peace sign (e.g. 'shalom', 'saanti', 'kapayapaan', 'damai', 'la paz', 'aman', 'salam', 'wetaskiwin')

Setting the Space

Cover the box with the length of black fabric, allowing it to trail at the front. Then, place the sand tray or planter box in the centre of the trailing fabric, with the basket of taper candles beside it. Place the large candle on top of the box, inside the hoop of barbed wire. Arrange a number of tea lights around this setting and light them. Finally, place the welcome or peace sign at the entrance.

Welcome

When the participants are ready, offer them a warm greeting. Then, introduce the theme and practise the songs for the prayer time.

Invocation for the Land and its First People

Light the large candle, and pause for a moment of silence.

Opening Prayer

> ### *Leader:*
>
> We gather before you,
> God of understanding,
> to pray for all those
> who are searching for a better life,
> those who are fleeing
> from cruel regimes,
> and those who have lost
> their homes and families.
>
> Scripture says,
> "the Lord protects the stranger."
> May the strangers in our country
> find refuge in you.
> May we have the courage
> to help you in this work.
>
> Amen.

Psalm

Psalm 61:1-4

> Please listen, God, and answer my prayer!
> I feel hopeless, and cry out to you from a faraway land.

Lead me to the mighty rock high above me.
You are a strong tower, where I am safe from my enemies.

Let me live with you forever
and find protection under your wings, my God.

Trans. The Contemporary English Version

Song

Under Your Wings

Under your wings, we find shelter.
Where will your wings take us now?

© Trisha Watts 1993

Reading

Matthew 8:20

Jesus replied, "Foxes have dens, and birds have nests. But the
Son of Man doesn't have a place to call his own."

Trans. The Contemporary English Version

Silence

Invite the participants to reflect quietly.

Reflection

Nasser's Story

I come from a small ethnic group in Libya and I love my
country. The government in Libya had taken away the freedom of my ethnic group. We are treated as lesser human
beings. I argued for the rights of my people for equality, for

education, for health care. The government threatened to take my life. I had no official papers. All the doors were shut in my face. There was only one window for escape. I got a forged passport and began to look for asylum in any country that may be able or willing to take me. I did not have the chance to join a queue of refugees. There were no other ways for me to obtain protection–both time and the government troops were catching up to me. A forged passport was the only way to save my life. It was either this or hand myself in to the authorities and place myself and my friends and family at their mercy. To condemn me for seeking this avenue to enter Australia is to condemn me for pursuing the right to live with dignity. My life and the lives of people for whom I cared were at risk.

Excerpt from The Truth Hurts, The Centre for Refugee Research. Published by the University of NSW, Australia.

Following the reading of this story, ask the participants to reflect on the following question:

- If you were Nasser, what would you have done?

Vigil of Light

Select two participants to read every alternate line of the following prayer. Then, select some additional participants to come forward after each line is read, light a candle and place it in the sand tray or planter box.

Leader: God of Compassion, we gather together as one people, in an act of solidarity, to light candles of hope for all those who struggle for the most basic of human rights.

Reader A: For those whose rights have been abused.

Reader B: For those who have fled their homes to seek refuge from persecution.

A: For those who face death, torture or violence from an abusive regime.

B: For those who cannot return home for fear of their lives.

A: For those who are forced to take desperate measures to find safety.

B: For those who are beginning their lives again in a foreign country.

A: For those who have lost their lives in the pursuit of refuge.

B: For those who have been persecuted for their political and religious beliefs.

A: For those who are born homeless, orphaned or helpless.

B: For those who live in refugee camps, waiting to return to their homeland.

Leader: Loving God, we pray for justice and mercy, healing and hope. Let us live in the spirit of compassion and understanding. Hear our prayers this day.

Amen.

Song

All We Long For

1. All we long for is a home,
   a place to rest our heads,
   where our children are free to play and grow
   beyond terrors that we've fled.

2. All we long for is a home,
   a safety from the storms,
   where the dignity of human life
   is valued and restored.

3. All we long for is a home,
   a space in which to breathe,
   where the stories of our lives are heard
   and our hearts can freely grieve.

4. All we long for is a home,
   a haven for our souls,
   where the gifts of peace and love are found
   and our future hopes unfold.

© Trisha Watts 2004

Closing Prayer

All:

Loving God,
we are all your children,
all part of the same great wholeness.
Some of us are settled,
others on the track to finding shelter,
all of us journeying towards
a universal truth
that heals and connects.

Give us the grace to see
our own need for refuge,
so that we may extend
a warm greeting to all those
we meet on the path.

Amen.

the naked voice

Introduction

The human voice holds immense power. It can both fascinate and delight, inspire and enlighten, liberate and fulfil, communicate and connect. A single word can bring a smile or a laugh, a gentle sigh can soothe and restore, a sharp cry can pierce the senses, and a beautiful song can bring tears to the eyes. The human voice lights up this world with colour and diversity, holding the potential to bring unity and harmony to all people. We should fill every place with our naked voices, undisguised by falsity or deception, but speaking words of friendship, comfort and goodwill. This prayer time offers us the opportunity to thank God for the great gift of our voices, and be inspired to use them to spread God's message of love amongst all people.

Resources

- collage of singers' faces (see below)
- tall pedestal or box
- length of black fabric
- four large candles
- tea lights
- bell or singing bowl with striker

Setting the Space

Prior to the prayer time, cut out some photos of well-known singers, composers and inspiring speakers from magazines, photocopied CD covers, etc. and create a collage on a large sheet of cardboard. Then, set the collage aside for later use. Cover the pedestal or box with the length of black fabric and place it in the centre of the space. Place three large candles at its base, along with some tea lights, and one on top.

Welcome

When the participants are ready, offer them a warm greeting.
Then, introduce the theme and practise the songs for the prayer time.

Invocation for the Land and its First People

Light the first large candle on top of the pedestal and strike the singing bowl
or bell.

Pause for a moment of silence.

Opening Prayer

> *Leader:*
>
> God of music,
> God of sound,
> God of the naked voice,
> we gather today to give thanks
> for the great gift and power
> of the human voice.
>
> We thank you for the ability
> to shrill in joy and ecstasy,
> and cry in pain and struggle.
>
> We thank you for the ability
> to yodel and sing playfully,
> to soothe wounds with gentle lullabies.
>
> We thank you for the ability
> to voice the never-ending chorus
> for justice, peace and harmony.

We thank you for the ability
to give sound to the mystery
of your presence,
the living Spirit in our midst.

Thank you for this generous gift.

Amen.

During the singing of the following song, carry the collage forward and lean it against the base of the pedestal or box.

Song

All is Wonder

In this moment, in this place,
all is wonder, all is grace.
In this moment, in this place,
we are one.

© Trisha Watts 2003

Litany of Great Voices

Light the second large candle and strike the singing bowl or bell.

Leader: We light this candle to honour the great composers for the human voice, who have lifted up and inspired us.

For the polyphony of Johann Sebastian Bach.

Response: Alleluia.

Leader: For the prolific hymnody of John Wesley.

Response.

Leader: For the choral magnificence of Palestrina.

Response.

Leader: For the operatic arias of Mozart.

Response.

Invite the participants to name some additional great composers. Then, light the third large candle and strike the singing bowl or bell.

Leader: We light this candle to honour the great singers who have soothed and raised our spirits.

For the soul of Ella Fitzgerald.

Response: Alleluia.

Leader: For the earthiness of Louis Armstrong.

Response.

Leader: For the blues of Billy Holliday.

Response.

Leader: For the passion of Maria Callas.

Response.

Leader: For the ecstatic chanting of Saint Augustine and Saint Ambrose.

Response.

Leader: For the activism of Joan Baez.

Response.

Leader: For the storytelling of Bob Dylan.

Response.

Leader: For the dreaming of Van Morrison.

Response.

Invite the participants to name some additional great singers. Then, light the fourth large candle and strike the singing bowl or bell.

> *Leader:* We light this candle to honour the great speakers of our time, who stir and challenge us.
>
> For the vision of Martin Luther King.
>
> *Response.* Alleluia.
>
> *Leader:* For the bold leadership of Nelson Mandela.
>
> *Response.*
>
> *Leader:* For the fierce compassion of Mother Theresa.
>
> *Response.*
>
> *Leader:* For the determination of Nugget Coombes.
>
> *Response.*
>
> *Leader:* For the tenacity of Aung San Suu Kyi.
>
> *Response.*
>
> *Leader:* For the understanding of Bishop Desmond Tutu.
>
> *Response.*
>
> *Leader:* For the passive resistance of Mahatma Ghandi.

Invite the participants to honour some additional great speakers.

Song

Justice Cry

Hear the voice of justice cry,
moving through our land,
ringing out over hills and plains,
linking hand with hand.

© Trisha Watts 1993

Reading

Colossians 3:16

Let the message about Christ completely fill your lives, while
you use all your wisdom to teach and instruct each other.
With thankful hearts, sing psalms, hymns, and spiritual songs
to God.

Trans. The Contemporary English Version

Reflection

As the reflection is read slowly, encourage the participants to add the sound effects that it indicates.

Leader: Once upon a time, there was a dark void, a deep darkness, a silence.

Then God created light and said, "This is good."

Response: This is good!

Leader: And from this light, God created sound.

There was moaning and groaning and sighing.

There were discords and strange sounds, confusion and chaos.

From this chaos, God created life, born into the sound of harmony and beauty.

It was born into the sound of choirs of angels, blending and yielding their voices, softly, gently, as a lullaby.

They became as one voice, all on one note, and this one song held every possibility, a wholeness and oneness.

God said, "This is good."

Response: This is good!

Reflections

Henry Wadsworth Longfellow
The human voice is the organ of the soul.

William D. Howells
It is the still small voice that the soul heeds; not the deafening blasts of doom.

Donald O. Bolander & Dolores D. Varner et al. eds. Instant Quotation Dictionary. (Illinois: Career Institute, 1972), 269

Silence

Invite the participants to reflect quietly.

Community Prayers

Leader: Loving God, we remember all the people who have lost their voices.

For those suffering abuse and living with daily terror.

Lord, hear us.

Response: Lord, hear our prayer.

Leader: For the mentally and physically ill.

Lord, hear us.

Response.

Leader: For those living under dictatorship.

Lord, hear us.

Response.

Leader: For the lonely and those who have lost confidence.

Lord, hear us.

Response.

Invite the participants to offer their own prayers to God, ending each with the above response. When all have been offered, gather the prayers of all present by saying the following prayer.

Leader: We offer you these prayers and ask that you hear them. Give us the conviction to speak up on behalf of the voiceless and sing up when hope is low.

Amen.

Song

In the Stillness

> In the stillness,
> there is a sweet gentle voice,
> calming the storms in the night.

© Trisha Watts 1993

Silence

Invite the participants to reflect quietly.

Thanksgiving Litany

Before beginning the litany, divide the participants into two groups, A and B. Ask each group to say every alternate line of the litany, as indicated below.

> ***Leader:*** Loving God, with all the choirs of angels, we give thanks for the empowerment that comes when we speak, sing, and are truly heard. We name some of these times now.
>
> ***A:*** Our voices are lifted when we are loved and included.
>
> ***B:*** Our voices are lifted when we are encouraged to share our gifts.
>
> ***A:*** Our voices are lifted when others listen and take us seriously.
>
> ***B:*** Our voices are lifted when we are delighted.
>
> ***A:*** We find our voices when we speak out against injustice.
>
> ***B:*** We find our voices when our stories are enjoyed and appreciated.

A: We find our voices when others take an interest in who we are.

B: We find our voices when we share our insights and wonders.

A: Our voices are raised when we are free to ask questions.

B: Our voices are raised when we sing in solidarity.

A: Our voices are raised when we willingly help and serve one another.

B: Our voices are raised when our uniqueness is cherished.

All: We join with the choirs of angels when we love, care and accept one another.

Leader: Gracious God, when we are lifted by your love, our hearts and souls are free to sing, and our voices rise on eagles' wings.

Amen.

Song

We Will Rise Up

We will rise up on eagles' wings,
lifted by your love.
We will rise up on eagles' wings,
lifted by your love.

© Trisha Watts 1993

Closing Prayer

God of All,
May the music of the spheres encircle our being.
May the heartbeat of love accompany our way.
May your Spirit inspire canticles and songs within us.

Amen.

Song

We Give Thanks

We give thanks for the goodness of love that is shared.
We give thanks for the circle around which we are fed.
We give thanks for the beauty of friends and family.
We give thanks, we give thanks, we give thanks!

We give thanks for tomorrow and thanks for today.
We give thanks for the journey and faith along the way.
We give thanks for the promise of Jesus with us now.
We give thanks, we give thanks, we give thanks.

© Trisha Watts and Monica O'Brien 2000

celebrating animals

Introduction

Animals are the delight of God's creation. Their grace, beauty, skill and diversity fill us with wonder and awe at God's power. In them, we see the reflection of God's great love, and are honoured that it should be shared with us on this planet vibrant with life. This prayer time offers us the opportunity to be inspired by the simplicity and generosity of animals, so that we might strive to live as they do, sharing the bounty of this earth and radiating the goodness of God in all that we do.

Setting the Space

Drape the lengths of coloured fabric on raised boxes, and place the animal carvings or sculptures on top. Arrange the greenery and foliage around their bases. Place the large candle in the centre and scatter the small candles throughout the setting. Use dim lighting to create a restful atmosphere.

Resources

- lengths of green, brown and earth-coloured fabric
- several boxes
- carvings or sculptures of animals (e.g. giraffes, elephants, dogs, etc.)
- ten small candles
- large candle
- greenery and foliage

celebrating animals

Welcome

When the participants are ready, offer them a warm greeting. Then, introduce the theme and practise the songs for the prayer time.

Invocation for the Land and its First People

Pause for a moment of silence as the large candle is lit.

Opening Prayer

Leader:

May all the animals be blessed!
Seahorses, buffaloes, majestic whales!
Such brilliance and beauty!
They put us in mindful awe
of where they came from,
why they're here,
and other mysterious questions.

Thank you, Great Maker, Shape-Shifter,
for your bounty and your beauty
that we see reflected
in this world of mystery.

Give us your guidance
and your protection,
so that we may be able
to live in the mystery
as the animals do,
with self-possession and humility,
taking only our share and no more,
for you have given more than enough for everyone.

Amen.

Song

Wild Creature Blessing

1. May all living things be blessed, with all their beauty shared.
   May all living things be blessed, not hounded or hunted.

2. May all living things be blessed, all creatures great and small.
   May all living things be blessed, honoured and adored.

© Trisha Watts 2001

Reading

Genesis 1:1,24,25b

In the beginning, God created heaven and earth.
God said, "Let the earth produce every kind of living creature
in its own species: cattle, creeping things and wild animals of
all kinds." And so it was. God saw that it was good.

Trans. The New Jerusalem Bible

Litany for the Animals

*Divide the participants into two groups, A and B. Ask each group to say
every alternate line of the litany, as indicated below.*

Leader: We give thanks to God for animals, for their inspiration and the reflection they offer of our inner selves:

A: Birds for inspiring us to fly;

B: Spiders for teaching us patience in spinning their webs;

A: Fish for beckoning us to the sea;

B: Sloths for teaching us to let go, to hang on in life;

A: Dolphins, otters and sea-lions for showing us how to play;

B: Giraffes for teaching us to reach out for what we need;

A: Kangaroos for inspiring us to cover great distances in a single bound;

B: Possums and owls for teaching us to be unafraid of the dark;

A: Fruit bats, platypuses and zebras for showing us that God has a sense of humour;

B: Porcupines for showing us that it is all right to be prickly;

A: Crickets, cicadas and frogs for inspiring our first string quartets and orchestras;

B: Stampeding elephants, cattle and horses for teaching us the power of drumming the earth;

A: Dogs and cats for showing us unconditional love;

B: Dingoes and wolves for absorbing the shadows;

A: Chameleons for showing us things are not always what they seem.

All: For all God's creatures, we give thanks.

© Alice Wheeler 2000

Song

Wild Spirit

Speak to my heart, Wild Spirit,
Speak to my heart, Wild Spirit.

© Trisha Watts 2003

Reflections

Meister Eckhart

We ought to understand God equally in all things,
for God is equally in all things.
All beings love one another.
All creatures are interdependent.

Matthew Fox, Meditations with Meister Eckhart. (New Mexico: Bear & Company, 1983), 26

Dögen

Coming, going, the waterbirds
don't leave a trace,
don't follow a path.

Stephen Mitchell, The Enlightened Heart. (USA: Harper Perennial, 1989), 50

Silence

Invite the participants to reflect quietly.

Community Prayers

Leader: Inventive God, we are in awe of your ingenuity and
sense of humour. You have created animals that playfully
teach us about the interdependence of all of life. We take time
now to pray for the animals of our world and the needs of our
communities.

For the myriad domestic animals that bring joy, companionship and love to family life, we pray.

Response (sung): May all living things be blessed, honoured
and adored. (From the song, *Wild Creature Blessing.*)

Leader: For the neglected and abused animals throughout the world, we pray.

Response.

Leader: For the people who work in wildlife rescue teams, animal welfare groups and with endangered species, protecting, healing and fostering animals, we pray.

Response.

Leader: For conservation councils and animal activists who watch over our water systems and advocate the rights of whales, sharks, albatrosses and other creatures of the sea, we pray.

Response.

Invite the participants to offer their own prayers to God, ending each by singing the above response. Then, conclude the community prayers by saying the following prayer.

Leader: Gracious God, we offer all of these prayers in your name.

Amen.

Closing Prayer

Leader:
Maker of all,
we thank you for all animals.
Without them,
our world would be a poorer place.

We thank you for farm animals
and those which are tame.
We are honoured
that they make their homes with us.

We thank you for wild animals,
those which fly and swim and hunt.
They remind us that your realm
extends far beyond us and our control.

We thank you for small animals,
those which collect and harvest.
We have so much to learn
from their tenacity and playfulness.

We thank you for insects,
those which fly and scuttle.
These myriad tiny treasures,
so perfect yet so frail,
bear witness to your abundance.

We thank you for large and lumbering animals,
in the sea and on the land.
We are humbled in the face
of their dignity and vulnerability.

We thank you for mysterious animals,
those that glow with light
or change shape and colour.
They fill our world
with enchantment and wonder.

We thank you for all animals.
Without them our world would be so lonely.

© Juliet Greentree 2000

Song

Grateful Heart

My soul proclaims with grateful heart,
my spirit rejoices, "How great thou art!"

© Trisha Watts 2002

money, money, money

Introduction

In today's society, life seems to revolve around money. Materialism and greed tempt us from every shop window and every billboard, and even from within our own homes. The air is choked with messages beckoning us to indulge ourselves, to seek something bigger and better than what we already have, to never be content with yesterday's fashion. In such a society, we need to be aware that money cannot buy everything. Possessions can never replace the gifts that God has bestowed on us; gifts like love, happiness, friendship, community, wisdom, kindness, self-esteem and inner beauty. This prayer time offers us the opportunity to reflect upon the temptation of money, to pray for those who are denied its benefits in this imbalanced world, and to ask God for the wisdom to make fulfilling choices for ourselves and others.

Resources

- different sized boxes and/or tables
- length of black fabric
- bric-a-brac, such as plaques, ornaments, statues, etc.
- large Bible
- bunch of flowers
- small candles
- large candle

Setting the Space

Arrange the boxes and/or tables at different levels and drape the length of black fabric over them. Place the bric-a-brac on one side of the boxes, and the opened Bible and the bunch of flowers on the other. Arrange the small candles throughout the setting. Place the large candle in the centre. Light all the candles.

money, money, money

Welcome

When the participants are ready, offer them a warm greeting.
Then, introduce the theme and practise the songs for the prayer time.

Invocation for the Land and its First People

Pause for moment of silence.

Opening Prayer

Leader:

Wise provider,
like nothing else, money can confuse us.
It is only a tool,
yet every benefit it brings can become a burden
if our attitude towards it becomes distorted.
In this way,
abundance can lead to greed and possessiveness.
Objects that are beautiful or well-made
can become poor replacements for self-esteem.
Even poverty or benevolence
can become a source of misplaced pride,
a way of defining who we are
in relation to others around us.

We come, as you taught us,
to seek child-like hearts,
as we think about money and all it is to us.

If we truly trusted in your providence,
we would never need
to be jealous of what we have.

If we truly loved unconditionally,
we would not hesitate
to share with those around us.

If we were truly in touch
with the needs of our hearts,
we would never try to substitute them
with something as poor as possessions,
which cannot speak,
cannot move,
and cannot love us.

Make us rich
in community, generosity,
simplicity and creativity.

Amen.

Song

Child-Like Hearts

If we truly trusted
with child-like hearts,
abundant love would fill our being.

© Trisha Watts 2003

Reading

Luke 12:32-34

There is no need to be afraid, little flock, for it has pleased
your Father to give you the kingdom. Sell your possessions
and give to those in need. Get yourselves purses that do not
wear out, treasure that will not fail you, in heaven where no
thief can reach it and no moth destroy it. For wherever your
treasure is, that is where your heart will be too.

Trans. The New Jerusalem Bible

Silence

Invite the participants to reflect on their regard for money. Encourage them to consider how they may best share their possessions with others.

Reflections

William Lyon Phelps

Real happiness is not dependent on external things. The pond is fed from within. The kind of happiness that stays with you is the happiness that springs from inward thoughts and emotions. You must cultivate your mind if you wish to achieve enduring happiness... for an empty mind seeks pleasure as a substitute for happiness.

Joshua Loth Liebman

The primary joy of life is acceptance, approval, the sense of appreciation and companionship of our human comrades. Many (people) do not understand that the need for fellowship is really as deep as the need for food, and so they go throughout life accepting many substitutes for genuine, warm, simple relatedness.

Thinking of You. (Norwalk, Connecticut: C.R. Gibson Company, 1977).

Song

Trust Greatly

Trust greatly in God,
and all shall be well.
Trust greatly in God,
and all shall be well.

© Gabrielle Lord 2002

Community Prayers

Leader: Generous God, we thank you for the many priceless gifts that money cannot buy, especially love, good humour, tolerance and wisdom.

Response: Make us rich in community, simplicity and creativity.

Leader: We remember the people, places and countries that are trapped in a cycle of poverty. Give us courage to speak out against exploitation.

Response.

Leader: Show us how to make honest and ethical choices in our financial investments, always considering the well being of others and the world.

Response.

Leader: Many of us struggle to make ends meet. Be with us as we explore ways to improve our financial situations.

Response.

Invite the participants to offer their own prayers for the concerns in their lives, ending each with the above response. When all have been offered, conclude the community prayers by saying the following prayer.

Leader: Gift–Giving God, may we always remember that we are priceless and invaluable in your eyes, regardless of our financial status.

Amen.

Song

Spring of Water

> You are a spring of water
> that never runs dry,
> that never runs dry.

© Trisha Watts 1993

Closing Prayer

Leader:

God of richness,
your abundance flows
into us, over us,
and through us.
Yet, most of the time,
we barely notice it.

Let us rejoice every day
in the freshness of a new morning,
in this gift of life,
the currency of energy that fuels us.
You know our needs and you supply them.
Let us relax in that certainty.

Let us bless you and rejoice at all times,
our gratitude growing every day,
knowing that our hearts and souls
are filled with your love.

Amen.

the ocean of love

Introduction

God's love is truly unfathomable. We cannot even begin to comprehend its depth or complexity, and yet we are blessed with it every day of our lives. Life is like one great ocean, the ocean of God's love. We are like droplets in this vast body, joined to every other droplet by the same inconceivable force. We are surrounded by love, overwhelmed by love, constantly in awe of a reservoir whose depth and width we cannot measure. This prayer time offers us the opportunity to recognise the importance of the changing tides within this ocean, and be confident that wherever we travel, God will always keep us safe.

> **Resources**
>
> - lengths of blue, turquoise, jade, lapis and sand-coloured fabric
> - sea shells
> - dried sponges
> - seaweed
> - tea lights
> - large candle
> - decorated 'talking stick'

Setting the Space

Place the lengths of fabric on the floor in a large horseshoe shape, with the sand-coloured fabric at the front, like a seashore. Then, place the sea shells, dried sponges and seaweed on the sand-coloured fabric. Position several tea lights on and around this setting, with the large candle in the centre and the talking stick alongside.

Welcome

When the participants are ready, offer them a warm greeting.
Then, introduce the theme and practise the songs for the prayer time.

Invocation for the Land and its First People

Pause for a moment of silence.

Song

Deep Waters

> Deep waters flowing,
> calling all to follow.
> Watching, listening, waiting,
> silence finds a home.

© Trisha Watts 1993

Opening Prayer

> *Leader:*
>
> Oceanic God,
> we gather here to ask you
> how to float in your love.
> Life came from the sea long ago,
> and in you
> all life remains.
>
> All-encompassing,
> all-embracing God,
> sometimes our lives crash and thunder around us
> and we founder and go under.

Teach us how to tread water
and lift with the swell,
how to duck under a breaker
that would spill us over the sand.
Teach us to ride with the flow,
your power providing us
with the energy
we need to go forward,
making changes,
living life to the full.

Stormy, tranquil,
sunny or dark,
you are the ocean
in which we swim.
Hold us in you.

Amen.

Reading

Genesis 1:1-2,20-22

In the beginning God created heaven and earth. Now the earth was a formless void, there was darkness over the deep, with a divine wind sweeping over the waters.
God said, "Let the waters be alive with a swarm of living creatures, and let birds wing their way above earth across the vault of heaven." And so it was. God created great sea-monsters and all the creatures that glide and teem in the waters in their own species, and winged birds in their own species. God saw that it was good. God blessed them, saying, "Be fruitful, multiply, and fill the waters of the seas; and let the birds multiply on land."

Trans. The New Jerusalem Bible

the ocean of love

Light the large candle during the following song.

Song

All is Like an Ocean

> All is like an ocean,
> all is flowing and blending.

© Trisha Watts 2002

Reflections

Fyodor Dostoevsky

> For we acknowledge unto you that all is like an ocean, all is
> flowing and blending, and to withold any measure of love
> from anything in your universe is to withold the same meas-
> ure from you.

Fyodor Dostoevsky, The Brothers Karamazor, Chapter 41, Part II. © 2004 Read Print

Meister Eckardt

> Into the sea all the rivers go, yet the sea is never filled up and
> still to their goal the rivers go.

Mathew Fox, Meditations with Meister Eckardt (Bear and Company, 1983), 57

Song

Protect Me, O Lord

> Protect me, O Lord, for my boat is so small.
> Protect me, O Lord, for my boat is so small.
> My boat is so small and the sea is wide.
> Protect me, O Lord.

Traditional Breton fisherman's prayer.

Silence

Invite the participants to reflect quietly.

Storytelling with the Talking Stick

A talking stick is a traditional prop used in story telling. Whoever holds the stick is given the authority to speak. Invite three or four participants to share their experiences of the ocean, giving each of them the talking stick in turn. They may interpret their experiences in either a physical or spiritual sense.

Community Prayers

Leader: God of the tides of our lives, we place the concerns of our fragile world into your hands.

Hear us, we pray.

Response: Hear us, O God.

Invite the participants to offer to God their concerns about the world. End each prayer with the above response. Then, conclude the community prayers by saying the following prayer.

Leader: Almighty God, we thank you for hearing the prayers of our hearts. Receive us just as we are and grant us peace.

Amen.

Song

Tides of Peace

Ebbing and flowing tides of peace,
make your home deep in me.

© Trisha Watts 2002

Closing Prayer

Leader:

Gentle Fisher-king,
like star reflections
floating on the water,
our souls lie
on the rippling tides of time.

Below us lies unfathomable love,
and above us infinite beauty.
We are carried
through the night on a dream,
surrounded by the music of silence.

O perfect navigator,
guide us through this immensity.
Do not let the darkness
overwhelm our frail lights.
Keep us moving in our little way,
rocking, rocking
with the waves.

Keep us safe.
Bring us to the morning
and our home.

Amen.

© Juliet Greentree 2002

winds of change

Introduction

Our lives have many stages of transition. As we grow and mature, we inevitably encounter the winds of change. In these uncertain times, we are often confronted with our fear of the unknown, our resistance to different ways. We feel too comfortable in the steady and unsurprising passage of each day, too absorbed by familiarity. However, God calls us to follow a mysterious path, designed to challenge our faith and love. It is sometimes cast into darkness or swallowed by storms, but the light of Christ always shows us the way to a better and brighter end. This prayer time offers us the opportunity to ask God to accompany us in these dark and uncertain times, leading us through the winds of change into a bright future.

> **Resources**
>
> - tea lights
> - large candle
> - seven lanterns or lamps
> - tapers
> - wooden stand
> - bookmarks, placed in a bowl
> - CD player and instrumental music

Setting the Space

Place the wooden stand in the centre of the space, and position the large candle on top. Hang the lanterns or place the lamps throughout the setting, and arrange the tea lights and the bowl of bookmarks at the base of the stand. The bookmarks should be printed with a copy of the first Prayer of Trust. Ensure that there is one bookmark for each participant. Light the tea lights.

Welcome

*When the participants are ready, offer them a warm greeting.
Then, introduce the theme and practise the songs for the prayer time.*

Invocation for the Land and its First People

Light the large candle and pause for a moment of silence.

Opening Prayer

> *Leader:*
>
> Protector Spirit,
> hold me in this shifting place.
> Like ice floes breaking up
> or earth splitting in a zigzag crack,
> my life is rapidly changing.
>
> This is new river; this is new ground.
> This is flash flood; this is no ground.
> This is the swing bridge over the abyss
> with too many slats missing
> and my feet skidding through to nothing.
>
> I can't go back: the slats crumble behind me.
> I can't go forward: there is only air.
>
> Spirit,
> hold me in this shifting place.
>
> Hold me
> while change unfolds within and without.
>
> Amen.

Song

In the Stillness

In the stillness,
there is a sweet gentle voice
calming the storms in the night.

© Trisha Watts 1995

Reading

Isaiah 9:1

The people that walked in darkness
have seen a great light;
on the inhabitants of a country
in shadow dark as death
light has blazed forth.

Trans. The New Jerusalem Bible

Silence

Invite the participants to reflect quietly.

Prayer of Trust

Step out into the darkness
and put your hand into the hand of God
that shall be for you brighter than any lamp,
safer than the known way.

19th Century Victorian Prayer.

Litany of Transition

Invite two participants, Readers A and B, to read each alternate line of the litany below.

Leader: Ever-present, embracing God, we often find ourselves in places of uncertainty. The challenges of constant change frighten us. In these times, remind us that you accompany us through the darkness and lead us into the light.

Response: We step into the darkness and take your hand.

Reader A: When we feel alone and afraid.

Response.

Reader B: When we leave our comfort zone.

Response.

A: When we are stripped of our belongings and identity.

Response.

B: When we are without a script, without roles to play.

Response.

A: When we feel dislocated and awkward.

Response.

B: When we fear that we may be thought foolish.

Response.

A: When we are unable to name what is happening in our lives.

Response.

B: When we fear that our new selves will not be acceptable or lovable.

Response.

A: When we lose confidence in the institutions we once trusted.

Response.

B: When we feel at risk or disempowered by the decisions of our leaders.

Response.

Leader: Loving God, be with us in the darkness of uncertainty, and guide us across the abyss. Your comforting love is a lamp safer than the known way.

Amen.

Song

See, I Make All Things New

See, I make all things new,
new as night turns to morning.
The Spirit is calling,
"I'm with you, I make all things new."

© Trisha Watts and Monica O'Brien 1995

Lighting of the Lanterns

Play some quiet instrumental music during the following prayers.

Leader: Ever-present, enlightening God, we place our hands in yours. You offer us an inheritance of unlimited love, for you are our Light!

Response: You are our Light!

Light the first lantern or lamp.

Reader A: You promise to be always with us, no matter which path we choose to take.

Response.

Light the second lantern or lamp.

Reader B: You help us to recognise the stages of transition as the stretch marks of growth, approaching fear with arms of love.

Response.

Light the third lantern or lamp.

A: You encourage us to take risks and 'go with the flow', replacing limited ways of thinking with fresh learning experiences.

Response.

Light the fourth lantern or lamp.

B: You guide us along paths that we never dared take, giving us courage and hope for new life.

Response.

Light the fifth lantern or lamp.

A: You lead us to the freedom of unconditional love and the richness of experience.

Response.

Light the sixth lantern or lamp.

B: You remind us that change is a gift of unlimited potential and possibility.

Response.

Light the seventh lantern or lamp.

Leader: God, it was you who said, "Out of darkness, the light shall shine." Let us receive your light with confidence.

Amen.

During the following song, invite the participants to come forward and each take a bookmark from the bowl.

Song

Light Will Shine

Out of darkness,
the light will shine.
Shine, shine, shine,
let your light shine.

© Trisha Watts 2003

Reflections

Rumi

I didn't come here of my own accord, and I can't leave that way. Whoever brought me here will have to take me home.

Philip Novak ed. Life: Spiritual Insights from the Great Traditions. (Surrey: Four Seasons Publishing, 2000).

winds of change

Richard Hooker

Change is not made without inconvenience, even from worse to better.

J.M. and M.J. Cohen ed. The Penguin Dictionary of Quotations. (Middlesex: Penguin Books, 1967), 193

Silence

Invite the participants to reflect quietly.

Community Prayers

Leader: God of change and transformation, we thank you for your sustaining love that enables life to be created each day. We ask that you shine your light into the places of deepest darkness.

We pray for the uncertainty in our fragile world.
For the insecurity caused by political and racial tensions.

Response: Give refuge.

Leader: For the anxiety caused by rapid technological change.

Response: Give perseverance.

Leader: For the illusions created by commercialism and materialism.

Response: Give discernment.

Leader: We pray for the uncertainty in our personal lives.

For the times we resist change by closing our minds to new experiences.

Response: Give vision.

Leader: For the times we fail to trust in ourselves, one another and your love.

Response: Give faith.

Leader: For the times we cling to old thoughts and patterns that limit our personal growth.

Response: Give courage.

Invite the participants to offer their own prayers to God, ending each with the response, "Give peace". Then, conclude the community prayers by saying the following prayer.

Leader: Loving God, grace us with renewed confidence in you. Hear our prayers this day.

Amen.

Song

All Will Be Well

1a. Let your body sway with creation.

Chorus:

All will be well,
all will be well.

1b. Let your spirit sing with elation.

Chorus.

2a. Joining hands with sister and brother.

Chorus.

2b. Sharing peace with stranger and lover.

Chorus.

3a. Praising God with joy and gladness.

Chorus.

3b. Stepping out with love and goodness.

Chorus.

© Trisha Watts 2002

Closing Prayer

Leader:

May the protective wings of the all-sheltering God
carry you through the winds of change.

May the healing wings of the redeeming Christ
inspire you to greet the winds of change.

May the soaring wings of the loving Spirit
raise you to fly on the winds of change.

Amen.

Song

Under Your Wings

Under your wings, we find shelter.
Where will your wings take us now?

© Trisha Watts 1995

the campfire

Introduction

The Holy Spirit is the fire from within, bringing the power of transformation and reinvigoration. When our spirits sag and our lives crumble, we are comforted by the Holy Spirit's presence, safe in the knowledge that our cries for help will always be heard. By the warmth of the campfire, we can ease ourselves into communication with God, letting the healing presence of the Holy Spirit penetrate deep within us. This prayer time offers us the opportunity to open our hearts to God's warming touch, and to be revitalised by the power of the Holy Spirit.

Setting the Space

This prayer ritual is best at dawn or in the evening.

Place the seating in a circle around the campfire, with the remaining items on a blanket to one side.

Resources

- outdoor venue where a campfire can be lit
- cushions, fold-up chairs, wooden stools, blankets, etc.
- clay pot, filled with soil
- pens
- sheets of paper
- sparklers for each participant

the campfire

Welcome

When the participants are ready, offer them a warm greeting. Then, introduce the theme and practise the songs for the prayer time.

Invocation for the Land and its First People

Lift up the clay pot and pour out its soil as the following prayer is spoken.

Opening Prayer

Leader:

All-powerful God,
each sunrise and sunset
reminds us of your constant presence,
awakening in each of us
the possibility for new life, new vision
and renewed energy.

Come and unite our hearts, minds and bodies,
as we seek refreshment from your Spirit.

Come and sit with us
as we listen for your fiery promptings this day (night).

Come and be with us
as we welcome your companionship and guidance.

For in this circle,
around this fire,
we are on holy ground.

Amen.

Silence

Pause for a moment of silence.

Song

I Am the Land

I am the land:
living, breathing,
dying, rising.

© Trisha Watts 2000

Reading

Exodus 3:1-2,4-5

One day, Moses was taking care of the sheep and goats of his father-in-law Jethro, the priest of Midian, and Moses decided to lead them across the desert to Sinai, the holy mountain. There an angel of the Lord appeared to him from a burning bush. Moses saw that the bush was on fire, but it was not burning up.

When the Lord saw Moses coming near the bush, he called him by name, and Moses answered, "Here I am." God replied, "Don't come any closer. Take off your sandals, the ground where you are standing is holy."

Trans. The Contemporary English Version

Invite the participants to remove their shoes and place them around the fire.

Silence

Invite the participants to reflect quietly.

the campfire

Ritual of Burning

Invite the participants to reflect on the concerns in their lives, the worries and anxieties that they would like to release. Then, distribute the pens and sheets of paper, and ask the participants to take some time to write down their reflections. When this is done, say the following prayer.

> **Leader:** Great God, we place into your hands our need for healing and reconciliation. Take our worries and our burdens into the fire of your compassionate heart. May its dancing embers be a sign of the transformation promised by your Holy Spirit.
>
> Amen.

During the following song, ask the participants to approach the campfire and throw their written reflections into the flames.

Song

Let Go, Release

> Let go, release!
> Let judgement cease.
> Let go, release!
> Open to peace.

© Trisha Watts 2002

Community Prayers

> **Leader:** Holy Comforter, we thank you for your deep presence with us. As a community, we remember our families, our work, our country and our world.

For the times when divisions and differences in our relationships seem insurmountable. May your gentle Spirit be the healing balm of peace, we pray.

Response: Hear us, Breath of Life.

Leader: For the times when our energy burns low and our lives appear in ashes. Grant us the humility to receive your kindling love, we pray.

Response.

Leader: For the times when firestorms sweep through our country, leaving it desolate. Make us aware that the seeds of new life soon burst open, we pray.

Response.

Leader: For the times we are faced with injustice, abuse, neglect, racism and prejudice. Ignite in us a fierce tenderness for the protection of all human rights.

Response.

Invite the participants to offer their own prayers to the Holy Spirit. Then, conclude the community prayers by saying the following prayer.

Leader: Holy Spirit, we offer these prayers in the knowledge that your love works in mysterious ways, far beyond our understanding. For this, we are eternally thankful.

Amen.

Passing On of Peace

Invite the participants to offer one another a sign of peace.

the campfire

Song

Holy Fire

> Holy Fire Spirit, create in us this day
> a spark with which to kindle love and play.

© Trisha Watts 2003

Closing Prayer

Leader:

> Our prayers fly up to you, Great Spirit,
> like sparks from fire.
> We know that you hear our intentions,
> yet sometimes your responses
> are not easy to discern.
>
> Give us hearts and eyes
> to penetrate beyond the surface,
> and ears to hear what lies too deep for words,
> so that we may find peace and delight
> and every other satisfaction
> in serving others.

Light a sparkler and continue:

> May your soul be inspired to dance!
> May your spirit find time to play!
> May you go out with joy!
> In the name of our Creator, Redeemer and Life-sustainer.
>
> Amen.

Invite the participants to light their sparklers from the campfire and offer blessings to one another.

dark night

Introduction

Sometimes in our lives, we feel surrounded by darkness. We feel trapped by loneliness and fear, isolated from love and warmth, overwhelmed by the hurt and neglect we have suffered. In these times, as our lives seem to spiral out of control, we need to be reminded that God is always with us in the midst of our pain and suffering. This prayer time offers us the opportunity to pray for help and recognise the comforting strength of the Holy Spirit.

Setting the Space

Create a large circle on the floor using the lengths of earth-coloured fabric. Place some cushions and chairs in a horseshoe shape around the circle, with the terracotta pot, bowl of flower seeds and ten candles in the centre. Then, place the remaining candle on another length of fabric at the entrance to the room. As the participants arrive, light four of the candles in the circle and the candle at the entrance. Play some quiet instrumental music and use dim lighting to create a restful atmosphere.

Resources

- lengths of earth-coloured fabric
- cushions and chairs
- large terracotta pot, filled with soil
- flower seeds, placed in a bowl
- eleven candles of various sizes
- CD player and instrumental music

dark night

Welcome

When the participants are ready, offer them a warm greeting.
Then, introduce the theme and practise the songs for the prayer time.

Invocation For The Land and its First People

Light one of the candles in the circle, and pause for a moment of silence.

Opening Prayer

Leader:

Bless us, loving parent,
as we gather in this space
made sacred by your presence and our own.

We thank you for our lives,
with all their richness.
We thank you for our friendships.

We ask for understanding
when life seems dark and full of fear,
and we shrink from embracing it.

Help us to accept
those with whom relationships
seem difficult or impossible.
Help us to embrace
those we do not understand.

Remind us of the seed
in the deep, dark earth.
It is in this darkness
that life begins to stir,

where movement into growth occurs,
and not till then
can the plant move into the light.

Help us to remember this
when we find ourselves
surrounded by our dark night.
Guide us towards the light and love of Christ.

Amen.

Song

Deep, Dark Earth

When life is dark and full of fear and doubt,
remind us of the seed in the deep, dark earth.
It is in darkness, life begins to stir,
and not till then can the plant move into birth.

© Trisha Watts 2002

Psalm

Psalm 131:1-2

My heart is not proud, O Lord,
my eyes are not haughty;
I do not concern myself with great matters
or things too wonderful for me.
But I have stilled and quieted my soul;
like a weaned child with its mother,
like a weaned child is my soul within me.

Trans. The New International Version

dark night

Reflection

Dark Night of the Soul

Leader:

In the dark of night,
led onwards by Love,
I crept out
while everyone else slept.

Light a candle in the circle.

Leader:

By a secret way
and safely hidden from sight,
surrounded by darkness
while everyone else slept,
I stole away.

Light a candle in the circle.

Leader:

No one saw me,
nor saw I anyone,
and no other light had I
except the one
that burned within my heart.

Guided by this light alone,
a light that shone
more bright than the midday sun,
I hurried to the place where my Beloved,
the one I know so well,
waited just for me.

Light a candle in the circle.

Leader:

Dark night guided me,
a darkness lovelier
and brighter than the dawn.
Dark night sheltered us,
as each of us transformed into the Other.

Light a candle in the circle.

Leader:

My Beloved lay sleeping on my breast,
caressed by me
and covered up with flowers,
as a soft breeze fanned us
from the castle's turrets.

Light a candle in the circle.

Leader:

Love wounded me,
and Love's gentleness
suspended all my senses,
so that I transcended my body
and all its cares.
I was transported
and I lay among the lilies,
my head on my Beloved.

Light a candle in the circle.

Saint John of the Cross, paraphrased by Gabrielle Lord

dark night

Song

I Have Loved You

> I have loved you with an everlasting love.
> I am constant in my affection for you.

© Trisha Watts 2003

Silence

Invite the participants to each take a flower seed from the bowl, as a symbol of hope in the darkness. Then, ask them to plant the seeds in the terracotta pot. Play some instrumental music as this activity is completed.

Once all the seeds have been planted, ask a participant to care for them over the coming weeks until they flower. The bouquet of flowers can then be returned to the group and used at another gathering.

Community Prayers

> **Leader:** When the night is dark and I feel afraid, hear my prayer, O God.
>
> **Response:** Shine your light.
>
> **Leader:** When the night is dark and I feel alone, hear my prayer, O God.
>
> **Response.**

Invite the participants to pray in a similar manner to the above. Then, gather the prayers of all present by saying the following prayer.

> **Leader:** God of Light, we thank you for your compassionate love. We offer you these prayers in the confidence of Christ, our Light.
>
> Amen.

Passing On of Peace

Invite the participants to join hands for a moment of silence.

Song

Light Will Shine

Out of darkness,
the light will shine.
Shine, shine, shine,
let your light shine.

© Trisha Watts 2003

Closing Prayer

Leader:

Spirit of Light,
sometimes it seems as though
our struggles are unbearable.
We feel lost and set adrift,
or imprisoned and overcome.
Our situations seem inescapable,
every mistake seems irreversible.
We are trapped inside
our fears and our loneliness.

Spirit,
in that place from whence you come,
possibility dawns eternally new.
If anything seems impossibly distant to us,
give us trust in those you provide
to accompany us through the darkness.

Give us trust in the path
when we cannot see our way.

Silent Guardian,
even the hardest road
still lies cradled in your hands.
Bring us safely to the light.

Amen.

© Juliet Greentree 2004

creativity and playfulness

Introduction

In this world brimming with life, we are surrounded by creative inspiration. Every creature, every plant, every mountain, every valley sings out with one voice, urging us to test our limits. Every creation of God beckons us to delve deep within the talents and gifts bestowed upon us, searching for new and brilliant ways to express ourselves and serve the needs of others. This prayer time offers us the opportunity to discover the creative power within every one of us, rising to the challenge of nature with an inexhaustible enthusiasm and playfulness.

Setting the Space

Lay the blank mandala on the floor in the centre of the space. Place the images of creativity and playfulness in the cardboard boxes, along with the quotations. Then, arrange the cardboard boxes, percussion instruments, basket, vase containing paint brushes and large candle around the mandala.

Resources

- large circular sheet of cardboard (mandala)[1].
- colourful images of creativity and playfulness, such as musical instruments and flowers
- large and small cardboard boxes
- quotations relating to creativity and playfulness
- percussion instruments, such as drums or maracas
- scissors and glue, placed in a basket
- paint brushes, placed in a vase
- large candle
- CD player and instrumental music

1. Mandala: geometric design symbolic of the universe, used as an aid to meditation.

creativity and playfulness

Welcome

When the participants are ready, offer them a warm greeting.
Then, introduce the theme and practise the songs for the prayer time.

Invocation for the Land and its First People

Light the large candle and pause for a moment of silence.

Song

All is Wonder

> In this moment, in this place,
> all is wonder, all is grace.
> In this moment, in this place,
> we are one.

© Trisha Watts 2002

Opening Prayer

> ### Leader:
>
> Creator Spirit,
> we gather together as your creations,
> each of us eager to be more like you,
> our Great Parent:
> brilliant, beautiful,
> wise and creative.
>
> Help us to be like little children,
> trusting in the moment
> and finding joy and pleasure in what we explore,
> expressing life in everything we do.
>
> Amen.

creativity and playfulness

Psalm

Psalm 139:1-3,13-16

O Lord, you have searched me
and you know me.
You know when I sit and when I rise;
you perceive my thoughts from afar.
You discern my going out and my lying down;
you are familiar with all my ways.
Before a word is on my tongue
you know it completely, O Lord.

For you created my inmost being;
you knit me together in my mother's womb.
I praise you because I am fearfully and wonderfully made;
your works are wonderful,
I know that full well.
My frame was not hidden from you
when I was made in the secret place.
When I was woven together in the depths of the earth,
your eyes saw my unformed body.
All the days ordained for me
were written in your book
before one of them came to be.

Trans. New International Version

Reading

Luke 18:16-17

Jesus called the children to him and said, "Let the little children come to me, and do not stop them; for it is to such as these that the kingdom of God belongs. In truth I tell you, anyone who does not welcome the kingdom of God like a little child will never enter it."

Trans. The New Jerusalem Bible

Song

Child-Like Hearts

If we truly trusted with child-like hearts,
abundant love would fill our being.

© Trisha Watts 2003

Silence

Invite the participants to reflect quietly.

Creativity Mandala Collage

Invite the participants to come forward and select some images and quotations from the cardboard boxes. Then, ask them to glue these to the mandala backing, as a celebration of their creativity. Play some instrumental music during this activity, and remind the participants to reflect quietly as the mandala is completed.

Reflection

George Vaillant

Like the birth of a child,
creativity compels us not to explanation
but to wonder and awe.

M. Bryan, J. Cameron and C. Allen, The Artist's Way At Work. (Pan, 1998) 3

Community Prayers

Invite the participants to join hands in a circle around the mandala.

Leader: Encircling God, inspire us to find creative solutions to the puzzling concerns of our world: injustice, racism, poverty, greed and oppression.

Response: Hear us, O God.

Leader: Encircling God, help us to recognise creativity and playful spontaneity as paths towards wholeness and well being.

Response.

Leader: Encircling God, remind us to protect, nurture and affirm the gifts that children bring: wonder, immediacy, open-heartedness and an ability to forgive and forget.

Response.

Invite the participants to offer to God their own intentions for the world. Then, conclude the community prayers by saying the following prayer.

Leader: Encircling God, hear the prayers of your people. Keep us mindful of your precious gifts of creativity and play-fulness.

Amen.

Song

All Will Be Well

1a. Let your body sway with creation.

Chorus:

All will be well,
all will be well.

1b. Let your spirit sing with elation.

Chorus.

2a. Joining hands with sister and brother.

Chorus.

2b. Sharing peace with stranger and lover.

Chorus.

3a. Praising God with joy and gladness.

Chorus.

3b. Stepping out with love and goodness.

Chorus.

© Trisha Watts 2002

Closing Prayer

Leader:

Creative Spirit,
your brilliance and your beauty are our own.
Teach us that each one of us
is a facet of your radiant playfulness,
each in our myriad different ways.

Joyous Playmate,
help us recognise that we are born
into an inheritance of riches,
that the materials we need for creative inspiration
are all around us:
the music of birds,
the colours of flowers,
the scent of trees,
the sculptures of shells,
the taste of fruits,
but most of all,
our pulsing hearts and world-ranging minds.

We live in a creativity workshop called the world,
and we give thanks and praise for this.

Amen.

the sabbath rest

Introduction

In the crazed busyness of our lives, when it seems that not even a second can be spared from productivity, we need to set aside time for the Sabbath rest. We need time to stop, to push aside our work and worries and remember that God is with us. We need time to allow God's soothing voice to refresh our souls. During this moment of peace, we can find true rest in the stillness that God creates for us. This prayer time offers us the opportunity to spend time in prayer and contemplation, and to be soothed by the calm of God's presence with us.

Setting the Space

Position the box or table in the centre of the space, and place the length of fabric and one large candle on top. Place the second large candle at its base, next to the Bible, opened at Leviticus. Scatter the cushions and tea lights throughout the setting. Finally, place the traditional and contemporary tools to one side for use later in the prayer time.

Resources

- large box or small table
- length of rust–red or earth-toned fabric
- two large candles
- Bible
- cushions
- tea lights
- traditional tools, such as a hoe, garden fork, hammer, chisel, etc.
- contemporary tools, such as a mobile phone, calculator, wristwatch, laptop computer, etc.

the sabbath rest

Welcome

*When the participants are ready, offer them a warm greeting.
Then, introduce the theme and practise the songs for the prayer time.*

Invocation for the Land and its First People

Light the first large candle and pause for a moment of silence.

Opening Prayer

Leader:

Loving Creator,
we gather here together
seeking the Sabbath rest.

Our lives are so busy, so crowded.
Life's riches sometimes give us indigestion.

Teach us how to find some stillness
even in the busiest day,
how to stop and catch our breath,
how to rest and refresh our spirits.

Teach us when to lay our tools down,
to take the time to breathe and be.

Show us how to bring our souls
back to a place of rest
within your sheltering wings.

Amen.

Ask some participants to lay the traditional and contemporary tools on the cushions.

Song

Sabbath Peace

Take some time to stop for a while;
rest your body, rest your mind.
Take some time for Sabbath peace,
letting go with ease.

© Trisha Watts 2002

Light the second large candle.

Reading

Leviticus 25:2b-4

When you enter the land that I am going to give you, the
land itself must observe a Sabbath to the Lord. For six years
sow your fields, and for six years prune your vineyards and
gather their crops. But in the seventh year the land is to have
Sabbath of rest, a Sabbath to the Lord; do not sow your fields
or prune your vineyards.

Trans. The New International Version

Song

Quies Sola in te Domine (Soul at Rest)

Quies sola in te Domine
(My soul is at rest in you, O God.)
in amore tuo domus.
(My heart finds its home in you.)

© Trisha Watts 1994

the sabbath rest

Silence

Invite the participants to reflect quietly.

Reflection

> *Leader:* The first word in biblical Hebrew used to describe God at rest is Shabbat. It means, 'he ceased his labours'. In the same way, God commands us to rest, to experience a touch of timelessness in our lives, to let the world be what it is for the day, to let go into rest.

Ask the participants to reflect on how they could let 'a touch of timelessness' into their lives.

Silence

Invite the participants to reflect quietly.

Reading

Leviticus 25:5-7

> It shall be a year of complete rest for the land. You may eat what the land yields during its Sabbath... all its yield shall be for food.

> Trans. The New International Version

Reflection

> *Leader*: The second word in biblical Hebrew is used to describe God at rest is Vayinafash. It means, 'he got his soul back'.

> During the Sabbath, we reflect on the 'crops' that have brought us good harvest and those that have failed to nourish us. We are given time to focus on the enjoyment, celebration

and nourishment that our labours bring. By allowing our souls to rest, we can reflect on God's plan for our lives.

Ask the participants to reflect on how often they take Sabbath time to contemplate and glean wisdom from stillness.

Song

Ground of Being

1. Ground of being,
   hear our cry for silence.

2. Ground of being,
   quench our thirst for stillness.

3. Ground of being,
   open ways for Sabbath.

4. Ground of being,
   lead us to still waters.

© Trisha Watts 2003

Reflection

Saint Augustine

You have made us for Yourself, and our hearts are restless till they rest in You.

Philip Novak ed. Life: Spiritual Insights from the Great Traditions. (Surrey: Four Seasons Publishing, 2000).

Community Prayers

Leader: Ground of our being, we remember our life-giving Mother Earth. For the times we have neglected or overworked her by taking too much, we ask forgiveness and the wisdom to allow her rivers to flow and her soil to fallow.

Pause.

Leader: In your compassion,

Response: We are renewed.

Leader: Ground of our being, we remember our earthly bodies. For the times we have dishonoured and stressed our bodies, we ask forgiveness and the courage to choose a more nurturing, respectful way of living.

Pause.

Leader: In your compassion,

Response: We are renewed.

Leader: Ground of our being, we remember our global community. For the times we have stolen the communal riches of other people, we ask forgiveness and the integrity to give back what rightfully belongs to them.

Pause.

Leader: In your compassion,

Response: We are renewed.

Invite the participants to offer their own prayers to God, concluding each with the above response. Then, conclude the community prayers by saying the following prayer.

Leader: Ground of our being, we offer you these prayers, knowing that you are always with us.

Amen.

Song

Under Your Wings

Under your wings, we find shelter.
Where will your wings take us now?

© Trisha Watts 1994

Closing Prayer

Leader:

God of the Sabbath moment,
into our lives, you bring the power of now!
This sacred moment, filled with life,
is powered by your presence.

Show us how to rest deep down inside,
so that when we run out to play,
we are refreshed and ready
for re-creation in our lives, our loves
and our communities.

Amen.

letting go

Introduction

Sometimes in our lives, we find it very difficult to let go of our burdens and troubles. We find it impossible to forgive, to reveal our inner pain, to heal our bitter wounds, to repair our fractured relationships, to accept our losses, to come to terms with our grief. Our hearts of stone weigh us down, stopping us from moving forward to better and brighter days. In times like these, we need to be confident that God's unconditional and everlasting love will release our hold on the past, giving us new hearts of flesh which radiate happiness and love. This prayer time offers us the opportunity to speak to God about the burdens and troubles in our lives, and pray for the courage to lift their weight gently from our hearts.

Resources

- large 'foundation' stone
- three medium-sized stones
- large candle
- tea lights
- rose petals floating in a bowl of water
- basket of smaller stones

Setting the Space

Position the large foundation stone in the centre of the space and place the three medium-sized stones on top. Arrange the tea lights, the large candle and the bowl of rose petals around this formation, with the basket of smaller stones to one side. Light all candles except the large candle.

letting go

Welcome

When the participants are ready, offer them a warm greeting.
Then, introduce and practise the songs for the prayer time.

Invocation for the Land its First People

Pause for a moment of silence.

Opening Prayer

Leader:

God our foundation,
in the time of letting go,
you strip us of all that we carry.
Our comforts, our assumptions
and our vanities fall away.

Free from our false sense of self,
we find our lives exposed.
Does our nakedness reveal
a heart of stone or flesh?

This day,
we lay at your feet all the things
that keep our hearts laden and tough.
In the silence that remains,
where there is nothing but our true selves,
be the solid ground beneath our feet.

Amen.

Psalm

Psalm 62:5-7

For God alone my soul waits in silence,
for my hope is from God.
God alone is my rock and my salvation, my fortress;
I shall not be shaken.
On God rests my deliverance and my honour;
my mighty rock, my refuge is in God.

Trans. The New Century Psalter

Light the large candle during the following song.

Song

Rest and Wait

Come, rest and wait in the wilderness.
Listen and see with your heart.

© Trisha Watts 1993

Reading

Ezekiel 36:25a,26

I shall pour clean water over you and you will be cleansed...I
shall give you a new heart, and put a new spirit in you; I shall
remove the heart of stone from your bodies and give you a
heart of flesh instead.

Trans. The New Jerusalem Bible

letting go

Reading

Matthew 11:28

Come to me all you who are weary and burdened, and I will
give you rest.

Trans. The New International Version

Silence

Invite the participants to reflect quietly.

*After a period of silence, pass the basket of stones around the participants.
Invite them to each take a stone to represent any heaviness in their hearts.*

Then, take some more time to reflect silently.

*Finally, invite the participants to place their stones on or around the foundation stone while the following song is sung. Ask them to anoint themselves
with water from the bowl of rose petals, as a symbol of God's gentle compassion and understanding.*

Song

Heavy Our Hearts

1. Heavy our hearts that are burdened,
tired our hearts that are pained,
weary our hearts that are broken;
come to our aid.

2. Comfort our hearts that are lonely,
melt our hearts of stone,
gentle our hearts with compassion;
come, make us whole.

3. Shelter our hearts by your loving,
tend our hearts by your care,
heal our hearts by your promise;
come, hear our prayer.

© Trisha Watts 2003

Community Prayers

Leader: Loving God, you take away our hearts of stone and give us hearts of flesh. Thank you for your unconditional love, acceptance and forgiveness, which enable us to begin again, revived.

We now take time to remember our families, communities and world.

For those who are living with the worries of illness or disease.

Give them strength, we pray.

Response: Hear us, O God.

Leader: For those who care tirelessly for others.

Give them endurance, we pray.

Response.

Leader: For those who are bridge-builders in the process of reconciliation.

Give them patience, we pray.

Response.

Leader: For the thousands of refugees and displaced persons who are searching for a home.

Give them hope, we pray.

Response.

Leader: For those who are educators, mentors and guides of our children and adolescents.

Give them inspiration, we pray.

Response.

Invite the participants to offer their own prayers to God. Then, conclude the community prayers by saying the following prayer.

Leader: Generous God, our hearts are turned to you. We offer you our humble prayers, knowing that you are closer to us than we can imagine.

Amen.

Closing Prayer

All:

Compassionate God,
hold us in your love, that we may not fear the darkness.
Help us be aware of your light within us all.
Gently lift us up whenever we fall down.
Call us by our names and we will turn to you.

Amen.

Song

Spring of Water

You are a spring of water
that never runs dry,
that never runs dry.

© Trisha Watts 1992

advent waiting

Introduction

Advent is a time of preparation and joyful expectation. We are filled with hope and open our hearts in wonder and praise at the coming of Christ. We unite together, waiting for the shining light of his love. As we hope and trust that Advent will come, we remember those for whom this light seems too distant, who have given up their seeking in despair. This prayer time offers us the opportunity to experience the love of God among us, extending from generations past to all eternity.

Setting the Space

Cover the tall box or plinth with the Hessian cloth and place the large candle on top. Arrange the large stones on top of each other to form a cairn , and place them in front of the box. Position a number of tea lights at its base. Place the small stones in a basket near the entrance, and invite the participants to take one as they arrive.

Resources

- tall box or plinth
- piece of Hessian cloth
- large candle
- large stones
- tea lights
- one small stone for each participant
- basket
- one taper for each participant
- CD player and instrumental music

Welcome

When the participants are ready, offer them a warm greeting.
Then, introduce the theme and practice the songs for the prayer time.

Invocation for the Land and its First People

Pause for a moment of silence.

Invite the participants to add their small stones to the cairn.[1] Then, ask them to take a taper to honour the season of Advent. Play some instrumental music during this time.

Opening Prayer

Leader:

When my beloved is coming,
I sweep the house.
I pick flowers and put them in every room;
bunches of lavender, sprigs of rosemary,
white linen, fresh bread on the table
and a jug of wine.
I light the candles, soft music plays.
When everything is ready,
I am prepared.
There is nothing left to do but wait.
All my work is done.
My heart is already open and ready to receive.
In stillness and in darkness I wait,
and my love comes to me.

Amen

1. *Cairn: Scottish-Gaelic word for a landmark or memorial site built from stones. See Genesis 31:45–49;*

"Collect some stones, and gathering some stones, they made a cairn...may this cairn be a witness between God and us this day."

Song

Grateful Heart

My soul proclaims with grateful heart,
my spirit rejoices, "How great thou art!"

© Trisha Watts 2002

Readings

Luke 1:46-49

And Mary said:
"My soul glorifies the Lord
and my spirit rejoices in God my Savior,
for he has been mindful
of the humble state of his servant.
From now on all generations will call me blessed,
for the Mighty One has done great things for me—
holy is his name."

Trans. New International Version

Mark 1:2-8

It is written in Isaiah the prophet:

"I will send my messenger ahead of you,
who will prepare your way—
a voice of one calling in the desert,
'Prepare the way for the Lord,
make straight paths for him.' "

And so John came, baptizing in the desert region and preaching a baptism of repentance for the forgiveness of sins. The whole Judean countryside and all the people of Jerusalem went out to him. Confessing their sins, they were baptized by him in the Jordan River. John wore clothing made of camel's hair, with a leather belt around his waist, and he ate locusts and wild honey. And this was his message: "After me will come one more powerful than I, the thongs of whose sandals I am not worthy to stoop down and untie. I baptise you with water, but he will baptise you with the Holy Spirit."

Trans. The New International Version

Reflection

Angelus Silesius (1624-1677)

If in your heart you make
a manger for his birth,
then God will once again
become a child on earth.

Stephen Mitchell, The Enlightened Heart. (USA: Harper Perennial, 1993), 88

Silence

Invite the participants to reflect quietly.

Community Prayers

Leader: We remember and pray for those who are struggling in this time of Advent:

Those who are sick and lonely.

Response: May they be blessed.

Leader: Those who are imprisoned and isolated.

Response.

Leader: Those who are homeless, without family or friends.

Response.

Leader: Those who have lost hope through too much change.

Response.

Leader: Those who are weary from the toils of the year.

Response.

Invite the participants to offer their own prayers to God, ending each with the above response. Then, conclude the community prayers by saying the following prayer.

Leader: Lord, we ask your grace upon us as we make these prayers.

Amen.

Song

Spark of Hope

1. "I am the light," says the Lord,
   "Come follow me into the light.
   I am the light, Jesus Christ,
   spark of hope in ev'ry land."

2. "I am the light," says the Lord,
   "Healing body, soul and mind.
   I am the light, Jesus Christ,
   Spark of hope in ev'ry land."

© Trisha Watts 2003

Light a taper from the large candle, and ask the participants to light their tapers from its flame.

Closing Prayer

Leader: Gathered together,

Response: We wait for the light.

Leader: Standing together,

Response: We trust in the light.

Leader: Praying together,

Response: We hope for the light.

Leader: Seeking together,

Response: We step out with the light.

Leader: Singing together,

Response: We are blessed by the light.

All: Amen.

Song

Day Star

May the hope of Christ rise up.
May it guide from near and far.
May the light of Christ shine out,
shine like the day star.

© Trisha Watts 2004

new year's peace vigil

Introduction

On the eve of a new year, when old dreams and resolutions have been fulfilled, it is again time to put our lives in perspective. As we reflect on the joys and successes of the past year, we are faced with a bright future, full of endless possibilities and challenges. At this time, God calls us to consider God's plan, a vision for the happiness of all humankind. We are each asked to play a vital role in this design, leading lives which mirror the love that Jesus proclaimed. This prayer time offers us the opportunity to commit ourselves to God's vision, and to surge into the new year with all the hope and promise that this brings.

Setting the Space

The amount of time spent with each section of this vigil is flexible. However, an allowance of two hours for the entire vigil is suggested.

Arrange the medium-sized candles in the shape of a circle, and position the four large candles at its compass points. Place the suitcase to one side of the circle, open and overflowing with the strips of white cloth. Place the small table near the suitcase, with the

Resources

- several medium-sized candles
- four large candles, coloured blue, orange, red and yellow
- large suitcase
- several strips of white cloth
- small table
- twenty felt-tipped pens (non-permanent)
- clothesline and pegs
- decorated 'talking stick'
- large bucket of water
- large table
- large sheet of paper
- crayons
- tea lights and holders for each participant
- sparklers
- CD player and instrumental music

felt–tipped pens on top. Set up the clothesline on the opposite side of the circle, with the talking stick and the bucket of water alongside. Then, position the large table some distance from the front of the setting, and place the large sheet of paper and the crayons on top. Light the medium-sized candles.

Welcome

When the participants are ready, offer them a warm greeting.
Then, introduce the theme and practise the songs for the prayer time.

Invocation for the Land and its First People

Leader: Let us bring our hearts and minds together to recall the blessings of this year.

Opening Prayer

Leader:

Holy Spirit,
we give thanks for the blessings of loving friendship,
good–hearted family members
and a country rich in space, food and beauty.

Let us gather these blessings into our hearts
and be still for a moment.

Song

Gathered on this Night

1. Gathered on this night,
   we pause to remember,
   pause to remember,
   pause to remember.

2. Gathered on this night,
   in heat of the summer,*
   heat of the summer,
   heat of the summer.

3. Gathered on this night,
   at close of December,
   close of December,
   close of December.

4. Gathered on this night,
   we praise our Creator,
   praise our Creator,
   praise our Creator.

In the northern hemisphere, replace with "in chill of the winter".

© Trisha Watts 2003

Naming the Blessings of the Year

Leader: We remember with delight our loved ones and friends who have travelled with us during the past year.

Response: Alleluia!

Leader: We remember with happiness our achievements at home, at work and in the wider community.

Response.

Invite the participants to name some of the blessings of the past year, ending each with the response.

> **Leader:** O God, we remember with joy the gifts you generously give.
>
> Amen.

Stories of Blessing

A talking stick is a traditional prop used in story telling. Whoever holds the stick is given the authority to speak. Using the talking stick, invite two or three participants to each share a story of blessing which they have experienced during the past year.

Song

We Give Thanks

> We give thanks for the goodness of love that is shared.
> We give thanks for this circle around which we are fed.
> We give thanks for the beauty of friends and family.
> We give thanks, we give thanks, we give thanks.
>
> We give thanks for tomorrow and thanks for today.
> We give thanks for the journey and faith along the way.
> We give thanks for the promise of Jesus with us now.
> We give thanks, we give thanks, we give thanks.

© Trisha Watts and Monica O'Brien 2002

Psalm

Psalm 116:1-2,5-6

I love you, Lord! You answered my prayers.
You paid attention to me, and so I will pray to you as long as
I live.

You are kind, Lord, so good and merciful.
You protect ordinary people, and when I was helpless, you
saved me.

Trans. The Contemporary English Version

Prayer for New Beginnings

Leader:

We bring to mind the losses of the year:
the loss of love,
the loss of work,
the loss of loved ones to death,
and days never to be lived again.

Loving God,
you make all things new.
Help us to release our hold
on old grief, old anger and old remorse.

Help us to allow space
for new visions and dreams.

Amen.

Ritual of Responsive Action

The following song may be sung during this ritual.

Invite the participants to come forward and take a strip of white cloth, on which to write their losses and regrets of the past year. Then, using the strips of cloth and the bucket of water, invite them to wash away their sorrows. The strips of cloth may then be hung on the clothesline.

Song

Let Go, Release

> Let go, release!
> Let judgement cease.
> Let go, release!
> Open to peace.

© Trisha Watts 2001

Reading

Genesis 28:15

> Be sure,
> I am with you;
> I shall keep you safe wherever you go,
> and bring you back to this country,
> for I shall never desert you
> until I have done what I have promised you.

Ref. The New Jerusalem Bible

Salute to the Angels of the Compass Points

Invite the participants to stand facing north. Then, light the blue candle and lift it high as the following salute is read.

> *All:* We honour the archangel Gabriel, who guards the north. May our minds be always guided by God's light.

Light the red candle and invite the participants to face south.

All: We honour the archangel Uriel, who guards the south. May our feet be always grounded by God's power.

Light the yellow candle and invite the participants to face east.

All: We honour the archangel Michael, who guards the east. May our right hands be always ready to bless and give.

Light the orange candle and invite the participants to face west.

All: We honour the archangel Raphael, who guards the West. May our left hands be open to receive and contain.

Leader: May the Archangel Gabriel, the traditional guardian of January, shine through the open doorway of this year and lead us into a new beginning.

Amen.

Reading

Ephesians 1:18-19

My prayer is that light will flood your hearts and that you will understand the hope that was given to you when God chose you. Then you will discover the glorious blessings that will be yours together with all of God's people.

Trans. The Contemporary English Version

Silence

Invite the participants to reflect quietly.

Calling of the Dreams

Invite the participants to reflect on their dreams and visions for the new year. As some gentle instrumental music is playing, ask them to come forward and write their dreams and visions on the large sheet of paper, as a community vision mural. When this task is completed, hang the mural in a prominent position.

Community Prayers

Leader: Gathered on the eve of a new year, we are mindful of the needs of our global family. As we light these candles of peace, let us offer prayers for the parts of our world that are divided and stricken.

Ask the participants to each light a tea light and place it in the circle, as a sign of peace. Then, invite them to pray for some of the troubled areas of our world and their concerns (e.g. Iraq, Afghanistan, Pakistan, East Timor, Zimbabwe, Thailand and Cambodia; war, aids, famine, poverty, detention centres and slave trading).

Song

Into Your Hands

Into your hands, we place our burdens,
into your hands, we place our trust,
knowing your hands are filled with mercy,
touching, restoring life.

© Trisha Watts 2003

Creed for the New Year

Leader: We envision a world where all people are cherished because they are precious in God's eyes.

Response: (sung) We hold this vision in our hearts and minds. (From the song, This Vision.)

Leader: We envision a world where each child is treated with love, dignity and respect.

Response.

Leader: We envision a world where the earth that nourishes us is held in respect and awe.

Response.

Leader: We envision a world filled with the power of love, enabling all things.

Response.

Invite the participants to share their own visions for the future, ending each with the above response.

Closing Prayer

Invite the participants to join hands in solidarity.

Leader:

Loving God,
once more the circle of the year has turned.
We find ourselves on the verge of a new beginning,
carrying with us our plans and hopes.
We cannot see what lies ahead.
We can only be certain
that things will not turn out entirely as we expect.

Yet, in this wonderful, sacred time,
as we move on from old realities
and prepare ourselves for the new,
we have the chance, once more,
to put our lives in perspective.

We ask ourselves:
Where are we going?
Are we achieving what really matters?
Do our goals still appear as they once did?

Often, we make choices
which consider only our own interests.
We forget that your purpose
is the only infallible support
for the fragile structures we build.

With this assurance,
the new year ahead
becomes a reason for great joy.
We can have the confidence
to commit ourselves to your vision,
and our lives to your purpose.

Let us take our faith in hand
and cross over the threshold to what lies ahead.

Amen.

Hand out the sparklers, to be lit during the following song.

Songs

This Vision

1. We hold this vision in our hearts and minds.
   We hold this vision in our hearts and minds.
   O, we hold this vision, we hold this vision,
   we hold this vision in our hearts and minds.

2. We build the future with our hopes and dreams.
   We build the future with our hopes and dreams.
   O, we build the future, we build the future,
   we build the future with our hopes and dreams.

3. We stand together in our living faith.
   We stand together in our living faith.
   O, we stand together, we stand together,
   we stand together in our living faith.

Repeat verse one.

© Trisha Watts 2003

Falling

Do not despair when you fall or grieve.
Falling does not hinder great love.

© Trisha Watts 1995. Inspired by the writings of Julian of Norwich,

A Time For Every Season

Trisha Watts

Chorus: There is a time for ev' - ry— sea - son— un - der hea - ven.

There is a un - der hea - ven.—

1. A time for birth - ing,— a
2. A time for weep - ing,— a
3. A time for tear - ing,— a

time for dy - ing— a time for up - root - ing,— a time to plant; a
time for laugh - ing— a time— for mourn - ing,— a time to dance; a
time for mend - ing— a time— for sil - ence, a time to speak; a

time for kill - ing,— a time for heal - ing— a time for ev' - ry - thing.
time for search - ing,— a time for los - ing— a time for ev' - ry - thing.
time for lov - ing— a time for hat - ing— a time for ev' - ry - thing.

All Is Like An Ocean

Trish Watts

All is like an o - cean. All is flow - ing— and blend - ing.

All Is Wonder

Trisha Watts

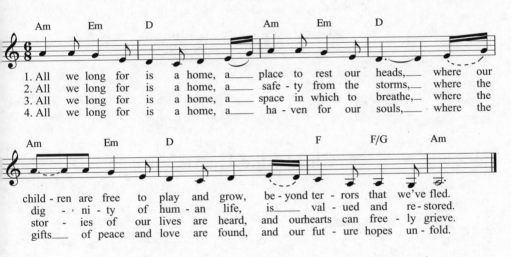

In this mo - ment, in this place, all is won - der, all is grace.

In this mo - ment, in this place, we are one.
(si - lence waits)

All We Long For

Trisha Watts

1. All we long for is a home, a___ place to rest our heads,__ where our
2. All we long for is a home, a___ safe - ty from the storms,__ where the
3. All we long for is a home, a___ space in which to breathe,__ where the
4. All we long for is a home, a___ ha - ven for our souls,__ where the

child - ren are free to play and grow, be - yond ter - rors that we've fled.
dig - ni - ty of hum - an life, is__ val - ued and re - stored.
stor - ies of our lives are heard, and our hearts can free - ly grieve.
gifts__ of peace and love are found, and our fut - ure hopes un - fold.

All Will Be Well

Trisha Watts

VERSES

1(a) Let your bod - y sway with cre - a - tion.
(b) Let your spir - it sing with e - lat - ion.

CHORUS

All wil be well,___ all will be well.___

2(a) Joining hands with sister and brother... [Chorus]
 (b) Sharing peace with stranger and lover... [Chorus]

3(a) Praising God with joy and gladness... [Chorus]
 (b) Stepping out with love and goodness... [Chorus]

Child-Like Hearts

Trisha Watts

If we tru - ly trus - ted___ with child - like hearts, a - bund - ant love would fill our be - ing.

Choose Life

Trisha Watts

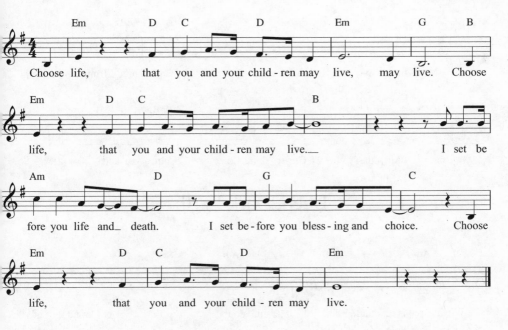

Choose life, that you and your child - ren may live, may live. Choose
life, that you and your child - ren may live.__ I set be
fore you life and_ death. I set be - fore you bless - ing and choice. Choose
life, that you and your child - ren may live.

Clear As Day

Trisha Watts

In the dark - ness, you are light, shin - ing clear - ly, ev - er
bright.__ To you the dark - ness is not dark, and the night is clear as day.

Day Star

Trisha Watts

May the hope of Christ rise up. May it guide from near and far. May the light of Christ shine out, shine like a day - star.

Deep, Dark Earth

Trisha Watts & Gabrielle Lord

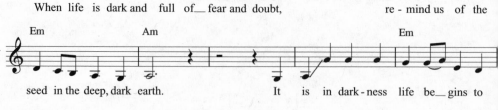

When life is dark and full of__ fear and doubt, re - mind us of the seed in the deep, dark earth. It is in dark-ness life be__gins to stir, and not til then can the plant move in - to birth.

Deep Waters

Trisha Watts

Deep__ wa - ters flow - ing, call - ing all to fol - low. Watch - ing, list - 'ning, wait - ing; si - lence finds a home.

Falling

Sung freely

Trisha Watts

Do not des-pair when you fall or grieve. Fall-ing does not hin-der great love.

Gathered As One

Trisha Watts

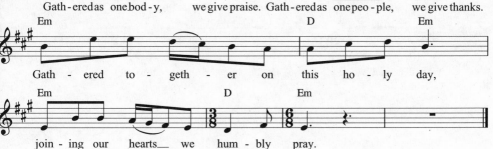

Gath-ered as one bod-y, we give praise. Gath-ered as one peo-ple, we give thanks.

Gath - ered to - geth - er on this ho - ly day,

join - ing our hearts__ we hum - bly pray.

Gathered On This Night

Trisha Watts

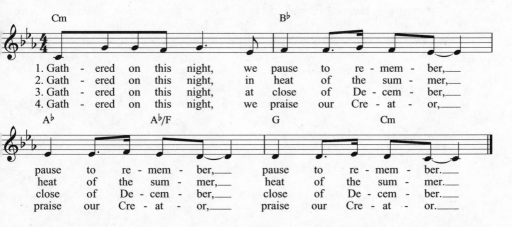

1. Gath - ered on this night, we pause to re - mem - ber,__
2. Gath - ered on this night, in heat of the sum - mer,__
3. Gath - ered on this night, at close of De - cem - ber,__
4. Gath - ered on this night, we praise our Cre - at - or,__

pause to re - mem - ber,__ pause to re - mem - ber.__
heat of the sum - mer,__ heat of the sum - mer.__
close of De - cem - ber,__ close of De - cem - ber.__
praise our Cre - at - or,__ praise our Cre - at - or.__

Give Us Courage

Trisha Watts & Monica O'Brien

1. Ho - ly Spir - it,__ teach us to__ for- give.__ Ho-ly Spi - it,
2. Ho - ly Spir - it,__ we turn our eyes to you.__ Ho-ly Spi - it,__ your

free us now to live.__ Give us cour - age_ to face each day. Give us

flame of love re - news!

CHORUS

wis- dom in all we do and say. Ho-ly Spir - it,__ teach us to__ for- give.

Grateful Heart

Trisha Watts

My soul pro - claims_ with grate - ful heart, my spir - it re - joi - ces: How great thou art!

Ground Of Being

Trisha Watts

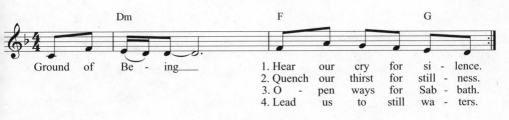

Ground of Be - ing___

1. Hear our cry for si - lence.
2. Quench our thirst for still - ness.
3. O - pen ways for Sab - bath.
4. Lead us to still wa - ters.

Heal Me

Trisha Watts

I___ will live for you a - lone; for you a - lone I'll live.

Heal me, heal me, heal me and let me___ live.

Heavy Our Hearts

Trish Watts

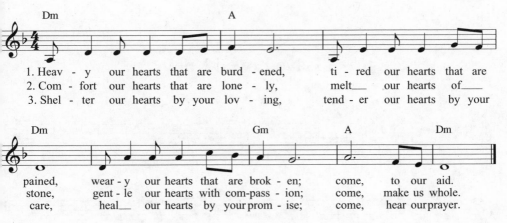

1. Heav - y our hearts that are burd - ened, ti - red our hearts that are
2. Com - fort our hearts that are lone - ly, melt___ our hearts of___
3. Shel - ter our hearts by your lov - ing, tend - er our hearts by your

pained, wear - y our hearts that are brok - en; come, to our aid.
stone, gent - le our hearts with com-pass - ion; come, make us whole.
care, heal___ our hearts by your prom - ise; come, hear our prayer.

Holy Fire

Trisha Watts

Ho-ly Fire_ Spir-it, cre-ate in us this day,_ a spark in which to kin-dle love and play.

I Am The Land

Trisha Watts

I am the land: liv-ing, breath-ing, dy-ing, ris-ing.

Icon Of Grace

Trisha Watts

May we see Christ's lov-ing face, may we be an i-con of his grace.

I Have Loved You

Trisha Watts

I have loved_ you with an ev-er-last-ing love. I am

con - stant_ in my af-fec-tion for_ you.

Into Your Hands

Trisha Watts

In - to your hands we place our burd - ens, in - to your hands we place our trust,

know - ing your hands are filled with mer - cy, touch - ing, re - stor - ing life.

In The Stillness

Trisha Watts

In the still - ness,_____ there is a sweet gent - le voice,

—— calm - ing the storms in the night.

Justice Cry

Trisha Watts

Hear the voice of_ jus - tice cry,_____ mov - ing through our_ land,

ring - ing out o - ver hills and plains, link - ing hand with_ hand.

Let Go, Release

Trisha Watts

Let go, re - lease! Let judge - ment cease, Let go re - lease! O - pen to peace.

Let Your Roots Sink Deep

Trisha Watts

Sing as a round

Let you roots sink deep;____ an - chor in a - bid - ing love.

Liberating Grace

Trisha Watts

Let us rise with you in lib - er - at - ing grace,____

____ with lives that know the pow - er of your gaze.
(free - dom in)
(heal - ing in)

Light Will Shine

Trisha Watts

Out of dark - ness__ the light will shine. Shine, shine,____ shine, let your light shine.

Like A Tree

Trisha Watts

Like a tree that stands by the stream,_ send deep your roots to the wa - ter.___

Be not a - fraid of the weath - er that comes: you will bear fruit if you trust in my love.

Love The Winter

Trisha Watts

Sing as a round

Love the win - ter____ when the plant says no - thing.

Our Lives Are Turning

Trisha Watts

Our lives are turn - ing___ and chang - ing view;_

time for the old___ to give way___ to the new.___

Praying As One

Trisha Watts

1. Gath - ered as one,_____ un - fold in us your mys - t'ries.__
2. Pray - ing as one,_____ you call us to our full - ness.__

Gath - ered as one,_____ en - fold us in your grace.
Pray - ing as one,_____ you heal and make us whole.

Protect Me, O Lord

Trisha Watts

Pro - tect me, O Lord, for my boat is so small. Pro - tect me, O Lord, for my

boat is so small. My boat is so small and the sea is so wide. O_____

Quies Sola In Te Domine

Trisha Watts

My soul is at rest in you,_ O God. My heart finds its home in your
Qui - es - sol - a in - te Do - mi - ne in a - mor - e___ tu - o

love. your love my heart finds its home in your love. Ooh___ my
mus___ qui - mor - e___ tu - o do - mus. O Qui

Rest And Wait

Trisha Watts

Rest and wait in the wild - er - ness. Lis - ten and see with your heart. Come!_

Restless Heart

Trisha Watts

I off - er you my rest - less heart,___ seek - ing un - div - id - ed love.

Sabbath Peace

Trisha Watts

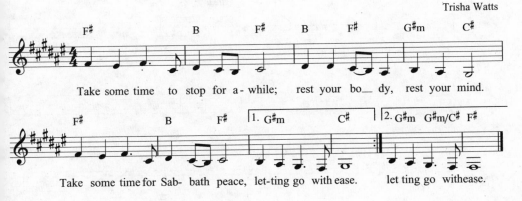

Take some time to stop for a - while; rest your bo__ dy, rest your mind.

Take some time for Sab- bath peace, let-ting go with ease. let ting go with ease.

Sacred Path

Trisha Watts

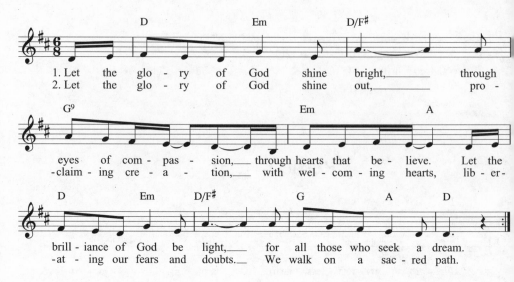

1. Let the glo - ry of God shine bright,_____ through
2. Let the glo - ry of God shine out,_____ pro -

eyes of com - pas - sion,___ through hearts that be - lieve. Let the
-claim - ing cre - a - tion,___ with wel - com - ing hearts, lib - er -

brill - iance of God be light,___ for all those who seek a dream.
-at - ing our fears and doubts.___ We walk on a sac - red path.

See, I Make All Things New

Trisha Watts & Monica O'Brien

See, I make all things new,_____ new as night turns to

morn - ing._____ The Spir - it is call -

-ing, "I'm with you,_____ I make all things new."

Seeds Planted

Trisha Watts

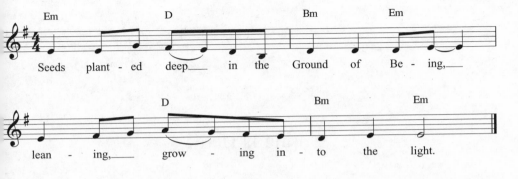

Seeds plant - ed deep___ in the Ground of Be - ing,___
lean - ing,___ grow - ing in - to the light.

Source Of Being

Trish Watts

Tribal Feel

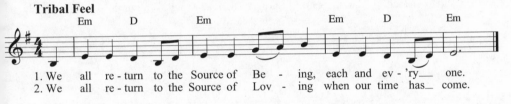

1. We all re - turn to the Source of Be - ing, each and ev - 'ry___ one.
2. We all re - turn to the Source of Lov - ing when our time has_ come.

Spark Of Hope

Trisha Watts

1. "I am the light," says the Lord, "Come foll - ow me in - to the light.
2. "I am the light," says the Lord, "Heal__ ing bod - y, soul and mind.

I am the light, Je - sus Christ, spark of hope in ev' - ry
I am the light, Jes - us Christ, spark of hope in ev' - ry

land." spark of hope in ev' ry land."
land." spark of hope in ev' - ry land."

Spring of Water

Trisha Watts

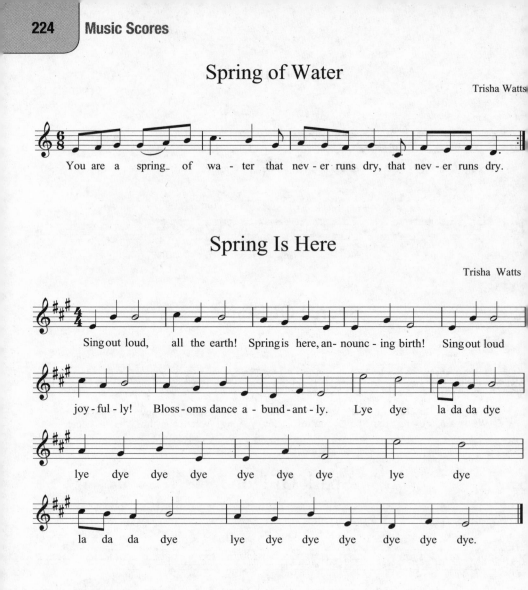

You are a spring_ of wa - ter that nev - er runs dry, that nev - er runs dry.

Spring Is Here

Trisha Watts

Sing out loud, all the earth! Spring is here, an- nounc - ing birth! Sing out loud

joy - ful - ly! Bloss - oms dance a - bund - ant - ly. Lye dye la da da dye

lye dye dye dye dye dye dye lye dye

la da da dye lye dye dye dye dye dye dye.

Surrender To The Earth

Trisha Watts

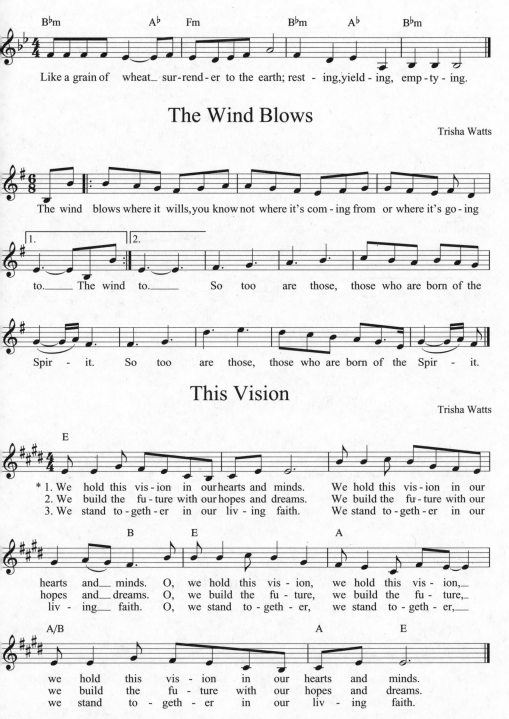

Like a grain of wheat sur-rend-er to the earth; rest - ing, yield - ing, emp-ty - ing.

The Wind Blows

Trisha Watts

The wind blows where it wills, you know not where it's com - ing from or where it's go - ing

1. to.___ The wind to.___ So too are those, those who are born of the

Spir - it. So too are those, those who are born of the Spir - it.

This Vision

Trisha Watts

* 1. We hold this vis - ion in our hearts and minds. We hold this vis - ion in our
  2. We build the fu - ture with our hopes and dreams. We build the fu - ture with our
  3. We stand to - geth - er in our liv - ing faith. We stand to - geth - er in our

hearts and___ minds. O, we hold this vis - ion, we hold this vis - ion,___
hopes and___ dreams. O, we build the fu - ture, we build the fu - ture,___
liv - ing___ faith. O, we stand to - geth - er, we stand to - geth - er,___

we hold this vis - ion in our hearts and minds.
we build the fu - ture with our hopes and dreams.
we stand to - geth - er in our liv - ing faith.

* Repeat verse 1 and the end.

Tides Of Peace

Trisha Watt

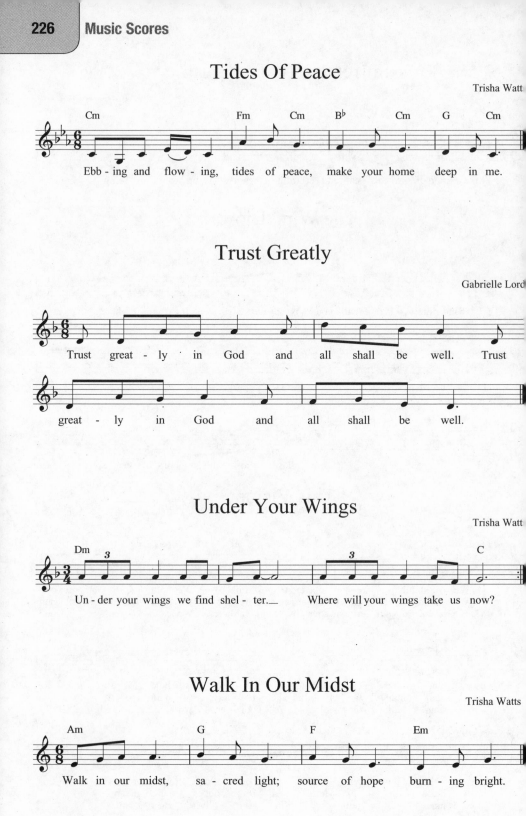

Cm   Fm   Cm   B♭   Cm   G   Cm

Ebb - ing and flow - ing, tides of peace, make your home deep in me.

Trust Greatly

Gabrielle Lord

Trust great - ly in God and all shall be well. Trust

great - ly in God and all shall be well.

Under Your Wings

Trisha Watt

Dm   C

Un - der your wings we find shel - ter.__ Where will your wings take us now?

Walk In Our Midst

Trisha Watts

Am   G   F   Em

Walk in our midst, sa - cred light; source of hope burn - ing bright.

We Give Thanks

Trisha Watts

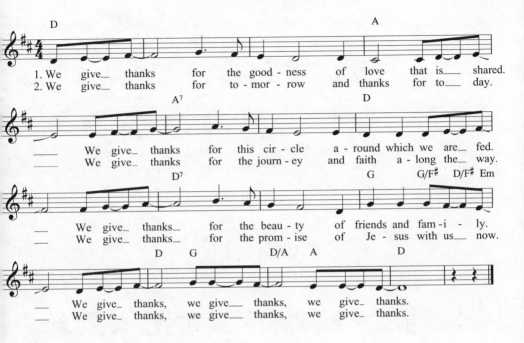

1. We give_ thanks for the good - ness of love that is__ shared.
2. We give_ thanks for to - mor - row and thanks for to__ day.

___ We give_ thanks for this cir - cle a - round which we are__ fed.
___ We give_ thanks for the journ - ey and faith a - long the__ way.

___ We give_ thanks_ for the beau - ty of friends and fam - i - ly.
___ We give_ thanks_ for the prom - ise of Je - sus with us__ now.

___ We give_ thanks, we give__ thanks, we give_ thanks.
___ We give_ thanks, we give__ thanks, we give_ thanks.

We Will Rise Up

Trisha Watts

REFRAIN

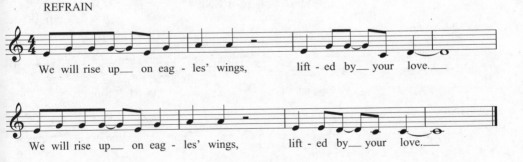

We will rise up__ on eag - les' wings, lift - ed by__ your love.__

We will rise up__ on eag - les' wings, lift - ed by__ your love.__

Wild Creature Blessing

Trisha Watts

May all liv-ing things be blessed, with all their beau-ty shared. May
May all liv-ing things be blessed, wild crea-tures great and small. May

all liv-ing things be blessed, not hound-ed__ and hunt-ed.
all liv-ing things be blessed, hon-oured and a-dored.

Wild Spirit

Trisha Watts

Speak to my heart,_ Wild Spir-it,__ speak to my heart,_ Wild Spir-it.__

Winter Is Past

Trisha Watts

CHORUS

Win-ter is past, the rains are o-ver and gone. Win-ter is past, the

flow-ers ap-pear on the earth.__ Come, my love-ly one, come see the blos-som-ing

vines. Hear the tur-tle doves coo-ing from the heights.

Women of the World

Trisha Watts

Sis - ters, we the mid - wives wo - men of the world, strong, a - live!

Sa - cred is the path we tread; bless - ings we will spread.

Yielding

Trisha Watts

Un - fold - ing love, o - pen and free,

lav - ish - ly giv - en, yeild - ing mys - ter - y.

song listings

The music scores are listed in alphabetical order.

A Time For Every Season
All Is Like An Ocean
All Is Wonder
All We Long For
All Will Be Well
Child-like Hearts
Choose Life
Clear As Day
Day Star
Deep, Dark Earth
Deep Waters
Falling
Gathered As One
Gathered On This Night
Give Us Courage
Grateful Heart
Ground Of Being
Heal Me
Heavy Our Hearts
Holy Fire
I Am The Land
Icon Of Grace
I Have Loved You
Into Your Hands
In The Stillness
Justice Cry
Let Go, Release
Let Your Roots Sink Deep
Liberating Grace
Light Will Shine

Like A Tree
Love The Winter
Our Lives Are Turning
Praying As One
Protect Me, O Lord
Quies Sola in te Domine (Soul At Rest)
Rest And Wait
Restless Heart
Sabbath Peace
Sacred Path
See, I Make All Things New
Seeds Planted
Source Of Being
Spark Of Hope
Spring Of Water
Spring Is Here
Surrender To The Earth
The Wind Blows
This Vision
Tides Of Peace
Trust Greatly
Under Your Wings
Walk In Our Midst
We Give Thanks
We Will Rise Up
Wild Creature Blessing
Wild Spirit
Winter Is Past
Women Of The World
Yielding